A Journal of the American Civil War

Managing Editor:
Mark A. Snell

Director, George Tyler Moore Center for the Study of the Civil War
Shepherd College, Shepherdstown, West Virginia

VOLUME SIX   NUMBER ONE

Published quarterly by Regimental Studies, Inc.

Subscription and General Information

Civil War Regiments is published quarterly by Regimental Studies, Inc., an affiliation of Savas Publishing Company, 1475 South Bascom Avenue, Suite 204, Campbell, CA 95008. Executive Editor Theodore P. Savas, 408.879.9073 (voice); 408.879.9327; (fax); MHBooks@aol.com (E-Mail). Managing Editor Mark A. Snell may be contacted at the George Tyler Moore Center for the Study of the Civil War, 136 W. German Street, Shepherdstown, WV 25443. 304.876.5429 (voice); 304.876.5079 (fax). All manuscript inquiries should be directed to this address.

Trade distribution and back issues are handled by Peter Rossi at Stackpole Books, 5067 Ritter Road, Mechanicsburg, PA 17055-6921. Voice: 1-800-732-3669; Fax: 1-717-976-0412.

SUBSCRIPTIONS: $29.95/year, ppd (four books). Civil War Regiments (Subscriptions), 1475 South Bascom, Suite 204, Campbell, CA 95008, or call 1-408-879-9073. Prepayment with check, money order, or MC/V is required. Institutions will be billed. Two hundred and fifty signed and numbered four-issue Collector's Sets for the premier volume were printed. Cost is $40.00ppd. Inquire as to availability. Back issues may be ordered from Stackpole Books (see address above). FOREIGN ORDERS: Subscriptions: $35.95/year, including surface delivery. Payment in United States currency only or MC/V. Allow eight to twelve weeks for delivery.

MANUSCRIPTS AND CORRESPONDENCE: We welcome manuscript inquiries. For author's guidelines, send a self-addressed, double-stamped business envelope to: Editor, *Civil War Regiments*, 136 W. German Street, Shepherdstown, WV 25443. Include a brief description of your proposed topic and the sources to be utilized. No unsolicited submissions will be returned without proper postage. Book review inquiries should be directed to Archie McDonald, Book Review Editor, Stephen F. Austin University, Department of History, P.O. Box 6223, SFA Station, Nacogdoches, Texas 75962-6223. (409) 468-2407. Enclose a SASE if requesting a reply.

Thanks to your support, *Civil War Regiments* has been able to make a number of donations to Civil War-related preservation organizations. Some of the recipients of these donations are listed below:

(LIFE MEMBER) ASSOCIATION FOR THE PRESERVATION OF CIVIL WAR SITES

RICHARD B. GARNETT MEMORIAL, HOLLYWOOD CEMETERY

HERITAGEPAC / CIVIL WAR ROUND TABLE ASSOCIATES

SAVE HISTORIC ANTIETAM FOUNDATION / TURNER ASHBY HOUSE, PORT REPUBLIC, VA

THE COKER HOUSE RESTORATION PROJECT, JACKSON, MS CWRT

AMERICAN BLUE & GRAY ASSOCIATION

APCWS 1993 MALVERN HILL/GLENDALE CAMPAIGN

Cover Illustration:
"Mower turns the Confederate left flank on March 21, 1865"
Harper's Weekly

Civil War Regiments, Vol. 6, No.1, Copyright 1998
by Regimental Studies, Inc., an affiliation of Savas Publishing Company
ISBN 1-882810-54-6

Contributors:

Roger A. Davidson, Jr. received his B.A. from Virginia Tech and his M.A. from Howard University, where he is currently studying as a doctoral candidate under Professor Joseph Reidy. Roger has enjoyed a long interest in the role played by black troops in the Civil War, and the 1st U.S.C.I. in particular, which is the topic of his dissertation.

Chris E. Fonvielle, Jr., who teaches history at the University of North Carolina–Wilmington, received his Ph.D. from the University of South Carolina. He is the author of *The Wilmington Campaign: Last Rays of Departing Hope* (Savas Publishing Co., 1997), an alternate selection of the History Book Club and the winner of the 1997 Clarendon Award. Chris makes his home in Wilmington and has recently completed a book on the battle for Fort Anderson.

James S. Pula is the Dean of the Metropolitan College of the Catholic University of America. The author of several books and articles, Dean Pula's latest contribution to the literature is *The Sigel Regiment: A History of the 26th Wisconsin Infantry, 1862-1865* (Savas Publishing Co., 1998).

Chris J. Hartley, a graduate of the University of North Carolina at Chapel Hill, is the author of Stuart's Tarheels: James B. Gordon and his North Carolina Cavalry (Butternut and Blue, 1996). He is also the author of several articles, as well as a new introduction to *A True History of Company I, 49th Regiment North Carolina Troops*, by William A. Day (Butternut and Blue reprint: 1997), part of the Army of Northern Virginia series. Chris lives with his wife and new daughter in Clemmons, South Carolina.

Mark L. Bradley is a free-lance historian/author residing in Raleigh, North Carolina, and a frequent speaker and battlefield tour leader. His first book, *Last Stand in the Carolinas: The Battle of Bentonville* (Savas Publishing Co., 1996), was an alternate selection of the History Book Club, and will be followed by another study detailing the end of the war in North Carolina.

Craig Symonds received a B.A. from UCLA and an M.A. and Ph.D. from the University of Florida, and holds the distinction of being the only ensign ever to lecture at the prestigious College of Naval Warfare. Craig is the author of numerous books, including *A Battlefield Atlas of the Civil War* (Baltimore: N & A Press, 1983), *Stonewall of the West: Patrick Cleburne and the Civil War* (Lawrence, KS: University Press of Kansas, 1997), and *Joseph E. Johnston: A Civil War Biography* (New York: W. W. Norton, 1992). He currently teaches history at the United States Naval Academy.

Table of Contents

Introduction

Mark A. Snell

Though overshadowed by the final months of bloody combat in Virginia, the campaigns waged in North Carolina during the last season of the Civil War hastened the demise of the Confederate States of America in a number of ways. While the armies of Lee and Grant pummeled each other around the defenses of Petersburg, the port of Wilmington was being closed by Union forces. The soldiers of William Tecumseh Sherman were also on the move, pushing their way northward from Savannah and leaving a path of destruction and desolation in their wake. Sherman's march tied up Confederate forces that could have gone to the relief of the Army of Northern Virginia. With the Confederacy's last Atlantic port now in Union hands and Sherman's army plowing through South Carolina virtually unopposed, the will of the Southern people to continue the struggle—and the war-making ability of their armies—teetered on the brink of collapse.

After the fall of Savannah in December 1864, U. S. Grant directed Sherman to join forces with the Union armies investing Petersburg. Sherman convinced Grant that if his command would be allowed to *march* through the Carolinas instead of making the trip to Virginia by ocean transport, his troops would be able to destroy railroads and other logistical targets along the way, as well as prevent previously-defeated Confederate forces from reorganizing. As Sherman was about to begin his campaign into South Carolina, Fort Fisher—the Confederate bastion on the tip of Cape Fear, North Carolina—fell on January 15, 1865, to a combined Union force under Maj. Gen. Alfred Terry and Admiral David Porter. Terry's "Provisional Corps" was joined soon thereafter by Maj. Gen. John Schofield's XXIII Corps from the Army of the Ohio, and together these forces (under Schofield's overall command) moved on Wilmington, which finally was taken on February 22.

Grant believed that the capture of Wilmington was critical to the overall success of Sherman's Carolinas Campaign. As Sherman moved inland through the Carolinas, Schofield would move northward with his army as a supporting force. The main objective of both commands was Goldsboro, North Carolina. Sherman's route would take him through Columbia, South Carolina, and Fayetteville, North Carolina, two important cities housing Confederate armories. Schofield's force, meanwhile, would move in the direction of the Wilmington and Weldon Railroad.

The capture of Goldsboro was important, says historian Chris E. Fonvielle, Jr., because "first, it was the junction for two coastal railroads (the Wilmington & Weldon and the Atlantic & North Carolina to New Bern) by which Sherman could be re-supplied and reinforced; and second, from Goldsboro Sherman could easily strike Raleigh, where Confederate supplies from Wilmington were being sent and from which point Sherman would be poised to strike the rear of the Army of Northern Virginia."[1] In his essay, "Making the Obstinate Stand: The Battle of Town Creek and the Fall of Wilmington," Fonvielle details the key land engagement of the Federal expedition up the Cape Fear River that led to the capture of Wilmington. Dr. Fonvielle, the author of *The Wilmington Campaign: Last Rays of a Departing Hope* (Savas Publishing Co., 1997), included new information and photographs unavailable when his book originally went to press last year.

A little-known Union regiment that participated in the final actions in North Carolina, including the capture of Wilmington, was the 1st United States Colored Infantry of the XXV Federal Corps. Roger Davidson, Jr., a doctoral candidate in history at Howard University, chronicles the exploits of this unit from the time it was raised in mid-1863 until it was mustered-out at the end of the war. Recruited primarily in the Washington, D.C. area, the 1st U.S.C.I. fought in several battles—including the attack on Fort Harrison, Virginia, during the Petersburg Campaign—prior to its service in North Carolina. His essay, "They Have Never Been Known to Falter: The 1st U.S. Colored Infantry in Virginia and North Carolina," sheds considerable light on the important role played by black troops in the Old North State.

William Sherman's troops were divided into two wings during the march through the Carolinas. The Left Wing, commanded by Maj. Gen. Henry Slocum, was comprised of XIV and XX Corps and a division of cavalry. The Right Wing, under the command of Maj. Gen. Oliver Otis Howard, contained XV and XVII Corps. The march began on February 1, with Howard's command departing from Beaufort and driving through Pocotaglio, Orangeburg, Columbia, and

Cheraw, South Carolina. Slocum's wing marched from Savannah in a direction that took it through Blackville, Lexington, and Winnsboro, South Carolina.[2]

Sherman's men encountered little opposition from the Confederates in South Carolina, who were desperately trying to gather together a patchwork of forces to stop the Union thrust. Lieutenant General Wade Hampton replaced Joe Wheeler as Confederate cavalry commander in the region, while Lt. Gen. William J. Hardee commanded a corps from the Department of South Carolina, Georgia, and Florida, and Gen. Braxton Bragg commanded the troops from the Department of North Carolina. The Army of Tennessee, a mere shadow of its former self after it had been wrecked at the battles of Franklin and Nashville, was commanded by Lt. Gen. Alexander P. Stewart. For overall command of the Confederate force, Robert E. Lee gained approval to resurrect Gen. Joseph E. Johnston, who had been relieved of command of the Army of Tennessee in July 1864, within the shadows cast by the spires of Atlanta. Johnston took over from P. G. T. Beauregard on February 23.[3] Johnston's most recent biographer, Professor Craig Symonds of the U. S. Naval Academy, discusses Johnston's role in the Carolinas in an interview conducted at Annapolis in the fall of 1997.

Sherman's army crossed into North Carolina during the first week of March, with Union cavalry under Maj. Gen. Judson Kilpatrick skirmishing with Wade Hampton's troopers on the 10th of the month at Monroe's Crossroads, near Fayetteville. On March 11, Sherman's two wings entered Fayetteville and destroyed the Confederate armory there the next day. The march northward continued on March 14, with Goldsboro slated as the final destination. In order to confuse General Johnston as to his intentions, Sherman sent the Left Wing in the direction of Raleigh. About twenty-five miles north of Fayetteville the main road to Raleigh branches near the village of Averasboro, with one road going towards Raleigh and the other heading eastward in the direction of Smithfield and Goldsboro. Upon reaching Averasboro, Slocum's wing would bear to the east. Meanwhile, the Right Wing left Fayettville and moved towards Goldsboro on a more direct route.[4]

Joe Johnston's new command was scattered widely in early March, and he needed time to concentrate his forces. Johnston ordered Lt. Gen. William Hardee to resist Slocum's advance at Averasboro. In addition to gaining time for Johnston, it was hoped Hardee's delaying action would help determine whether Slocum's wing was headed for Raleigh or Goldsboro.[5] In "Battle in the Swamp: Cogswell's Brigade at Averasboro," James S. Pula, Dean of the Metropolitan College of Catholic University, discusses the role of Brig. Gen. William Cogswell's brigade of the Third Division, XX Corps, at the battle fought on March

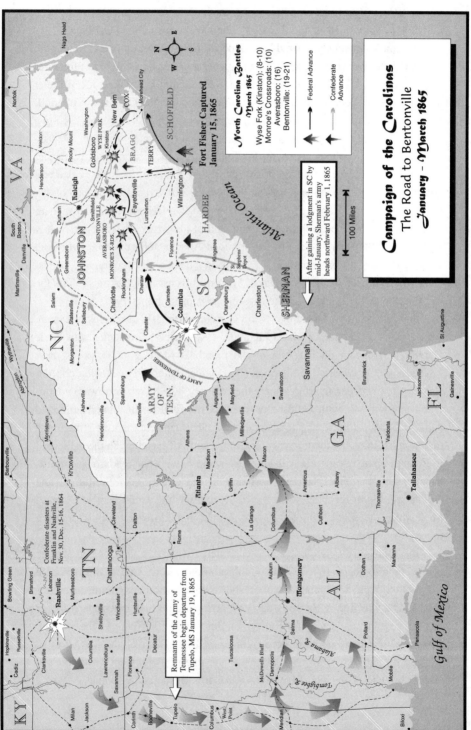

Mark A. Moore

Campaign of the Carolinas
The Road to Bentonville
January – March 1865

North Carolina Battles
March 1865

Wyse Fork (Kinston): (8-10)
Monroe's Crossroads: (10)
Averasboro: (16)
Bentonville: (19-21)

⟵ Federal Advance

⟵ Confederate Advance

After gaining a lodgment in SC by mid-January, Sherman's army heads northward February 1, 1865

⊢—— 100 Miles ——⊣

Fort Fisher Captured
January 15, 1865

Remnants of the Army of Tennessee begin departure from Tupelo, MS January 19, 1865

Confederate disasters at Franklin and Nashville, Nov. 30, Dec. 15-16, 1864

15-16. "In the end, Hardee's delaying action did not accomplish its purpose," concludes Pula, the author of a new book about the 26th Wisconsin Infantry, one of Cogswell's regiments. "The Federal success was due in no small part to Cogswell's brigade."

Hardee suffered over 800 casualties at Averasboro although he was able to buy Johnston a handful of critical hours. Slocum's delay increased the distance separating the two wings of Sherman's army, giving Johnston a final opportunity to concentrate his command and attack the Left Wing with superior numbers before the Right Wing could come to its rescue. On March 19 Johnston struck the head of Slocum's marching column at the hamlet of Bentonville. Although the Confederates met with initial success, stubborn Federal resistance by the XIV and XX Corps prevented a Federal collapse. When the Right Wing under O. O. Howard arrived the following morning, however, Johnston was outnumbered three to one. Two additional days of skirmishing and fighting ensued before Johnston withdrew his battered force on March 21. With Johnston brushed aside, Sherman continued his march to Goldsboro, where he arrived three days later.[6]

Mark L. Bradley, author of *Last Stand in the Carolinas: The Battle of Bentonville* (Campbell, 1995), has edited two previously unpublished Confederate documents concerning this battle. The first is an after-action report penned by Maj. Gen. Henry D. Clayton, a division commander in the Army of Tennessee, while the second is a reminiscence by Col. Henry Bunn, a brigade commander in the same army. "They provide two unique views of the same battle," writes Bradley, "and from vantage points that were probably never more than several hundred yards apart."

Bentonville proved to be the last major action in North Carolina, but the end of the war still was several weeks away. On last day of the fighting at Bentonville, Maj. Gen. George Stoneman's Federal cavalry division left Knoxville, Tennessee, for a raid of destruction through western North Carolina and southwestern Virginia. Chris Hartley examines the conduct and results of one of the longest cavalry raids in history in "'Like An Avalanche': George Stoneman's 1865 Raid." Hartley concludes that "Stoneman's raiders eliminated the supplies, reinforcements, and line of retreat that Joe Johnston and Robert E. Lee would have required to continue the struggle. Without such an infrastructure, the rebellion died." And with Lee's surrender at Appomattox on April 9 and Johnston's capitulation at Bennett Place seventeen days later, the rebellion did indeed die.

This issue of *Civil War Regiments* brings to light some of the lesser-known episodes of the final months of the war. "North Carolina: The Final Campaigns," introduces obscure or previously overlooked organizations, discusses in some detail various battles and skirmishes, and provides readers with a deeper understanding of the overall strategic picture in Virginia and the Carolinas as the conflict drew to a close. Its publication adds contributes one more piece to the mosaic of our unique Civil War.

Notes

1. Chris E. Fonvielle, Jr., *Last Rays of a Departing Hope: The Wilmington Campaign* (Savas Publishing Co., 1997), 332.

2. Joseph T. Glatthaar, *The March to the Sea and Beyond: Sherman's Troops in the Savannah and Carolinas Campaigns* (New York, 1985), 12.

3. Ibid.; Mark A. Moore, *Moore's Historical Guide to the Battle of Bentonville* (Savas Publishing Co., 1997), 3.

4. Ibid., 9.

5. Ibid.

6. Glatthaar, *The March to the Sea and Beyond*, 12-13.

" We are too patriotic to our race not to distinguish ourselves . . . ."

"THEY HAVE NEVER BEEN KNOWN TO FALTER"

The First United States Colored Infantry in Virginia and North Carolina

Roger A. Davidson, Jr.

Historians estimate that approximately 180,000 black Americans served in the United States Army during the Civil War. Although they came from all across the Union and Confederate states and shared varied backgrounds, these men had two things in common: the desire to fight for the freedom of their race and the chance to prove they deserved rights of U. S. citizenship. When analyzing their Civil War military experiences, the circumstances under which they served are very significant. Because of the notion that black men could not perform well in combat, fatigue duty and rearguard tasks filled the experiences of most black soldiers. Nonetheless, some black regiments served in areas marked by frequent combat and disproved the prevailing stigma of inferiority.

Of the approximately 166 black regiments raised, historians have concentrated only on a famous few, such as the 54th Massachusetts and 1st South Carolina. This is due, in part, because historians tend to focus on a regiment's relation to certain notable political or military events, and ignore the possibility of their usefulness in regional histories. Consequentially, there is much still to be discovered about the martial exploits of the Union army's black regiments.[1]

The First United States Colored Infantry (1st U.S.C.I.), initially designated the First District of Columbia Colored Volunteer Infantry, is one of the lesser known regiments that offers a wealth of information on the black military experience. In addition, a study of this unit tells us much about the history of Civil War-era Washington, D.C., Virginia, and North Carolina. The 1st U.S.C.I. participated in 13 battles in two major campaigns in Virginia and North Carolina and served as an occupation force in the latter state. The regiment's ranks included freemen and freedmen, Northerners and Southerners, most of whom lived in and around the District of Columbia at their time of enlistment.

In order to appreciate the experiences of the 1st U.S.C.I., it is necessary to understand the political, social, and economic environment of Washington, D.C., the regiment's home city. In 1860, Washington was a bustling Southern city with a population of approximately 61,000 people, which included 9,209 free blacks and 1,744 slaves. Nearly forty percent of the free-black population was literate. Most worked as skilled laborers and domestic servants, although a fortunate few held clerical positions with the Federal government. The slave population consisted mainly of house servants and artisans. Though tolerant of the large free-black population, the local government strictly enforced the city's black codes and the federal fugitive slave law. The presence of professional slave catchers and the opportunity they enjoyed to profit from the sale of captured blacks—both fugitive slave as well as free born—restricted the liberties of Washington's freemen.[2]

Despite certain restrictions and dangers, free and enslaved African Americans exploited many employment and social opportunities in antebellum Washington. Free blacks readily found employment at tasks judged too menial for whites. Despite their low socioeconomic status, these jobs provided money for the bare necessities and sometimes enough for a comfortable subsistence. For the skilled, educated, and ambitious, Washington offered them the opportunity to join a small and somewhat prosperous black elite. The large free-black population created a social environment that supported black churches, private schools, social clubs, and literary societies. Some slaves could hire out their services and mingle with the free population. In some instances, slave owners even allowed those bondsmen who worked away from home to live in the free black community.[3]

From the early nineteenth century, the opportunities afforded to black Washingtonians attracted free blacks and fugitive slaves from neighboring Maryland and Virginia. Fugitives easily blended in to the sizable free-black population in Washington. Some of the men who would join the 1st U.S.C.I. belonged to families that had migrated to antebellum Washington in order to take advantage of the social and economic opportunities that the city provided.

For example, the family of Charles Gurtrige moved from Maryland to Washington in 1845, after Gurtrige's father purchased his family's freedom from Thomas Bell of adjacent Prince George's County. Prior to the war, Gurtrige worked as a carpenter in Washington and Prince George's County. Similarly, George W. Hatton's father, a free Maryland farmer, purchased his family in the 1840s. Hatton traveled to Washington in 1858 in search of employment, and landed a job as an apothecary clerk. The family of Richard Henderson, escaped from a Maryland farm when Richard was an infant and made their way to Washington in the mid-1840s. They established a new life in the capital city under the assumed name of Smith. When Richard reached working age just before the war he took employment as a brick maker in the Washington brickyard.[4]

The outbreak of civil war in April 1861 provided the impetus for an ever increasing number of fugitive slaves to seek asylum in Washington. The maneuvers of contending armies and the actions of anti-slavery minded Union soldiers provided the initial avenues for escape. Abolitionist soldiers offered the fugitives protection and sustenance. Union soldiers who cared little for blacks but saw a chance to slight slave holders provided fugitives with asylum and employment as servants. Yet safety for fugitives was not always assured; some military commanders honored Lincoln's unofficial pledge of noninterference with slavery and returned or denied refuge to runaway slaves.[5]

The increasing number of fugitives fleeing to Union camps coupled with the protests of loyal slave holders forced the army, the Lincoln administration, and Congress to take an official stance with regard to escaped slaves. At Fort Monroe, Virginia, Maj. Gen. Benjamin Butler provided an expedient and politically sound solution. In May 1861, Butler refused to return fugitives because of the disloyalty of Virginia slave holders and the use of slave labor to build Confederate fortifications. Butler justified his actions by labeling the fugitives as "contraband of war." Major General Joseph K. Mansfield, commander of the Department of Washington, adopted Butler's position in July 1861 and ordered civil and military authorities in Washington to hold the fugitive slaves of "disloyal" Virginians as contraband of war and use them as laborers. Taking heart from Butler's actions, Congress passed the First Confiscation Act in August. This act officially sanctioned the confiscation of slaves used as laborers in the Confederate war effort and thus nullified the claims for fugitives made by slave holders from disloyal states. Butler's contraband policy and the First Confiscation Act became the catalyst for the drastic demographic and political changes that occurred in Washington in 1862.[6]

War-related labor shortages and General Mansfield's contraband policy created many employment opportunities for African Americans as servants, hack drivers, bootblacks, barbers, teamsters, and waiters. There was a need for laborers to build fortifications around Washington, as well as a demand for skilled artisans to replace the white men who had joined the army. The army's commissary and quartermaster corps required lots of strong backs and thus became the primary employers of contrabands. Military laborers earned between $10 and $25 monthly, depending upon their skills. Furthermore, the large number of soldiers and military contractors in Washington provided opportunities for blacks to gain employment as cooks and personal attendants. Over the course of 1862, the Republican-controlled Congress and President Lincoln took a series of steps that resulted in an ever greater influx of African Americans to Washington.[7]

On April 11, 1862, Congress passed a bill prohibiting slavery in Washington, D.C., and provided for the compensated emancipation of the city's slaves. This law, for the most part a symbolic gesture of freedom, did end slavery in the capital of a free nation. In the same month, the city's legislature rescinded Washington's black codes, which allowed the African American population a chance to enjoy a greater sense of citizenship and a more independent social life. In July, Congress passed the Second Confiscation Act which effectively freed any slave within the Union lines. The Second Confiscation Act declared the fugitive slaves of "disloyal" masters forever free and forbade persons in the Federal service to question the validity of a slave's claim to freedom. During the same session, Congress passed the Militia Act of 1862, which allowed the recruitment of blacks for military and naval service. Finally, on September 22, 1862, Lincoln announced that he would issue an Emancipation Proclamation on January 1, 1863, freeing the slaves in the rebellious states. The result of this radical legislation was a greater influx of fugitive slaves from loyal Maryland and disloyal Virginia, as well as free blacks from other states.[8]

Movements of the opposing armies and military engagements provided the ideal circumstances for some slaves to escape to Washington. Francis Marshall, for instance, labored as a slave near Malvern Hill, Virginia, until the Seven Days' Battles. The last of these actions, which took place at Malvern Hill, brought him in contact with the 5th New York Volunteer Infantry. Marshall became the body servant of Col. Gouvernor K. Warren, the regiment's commander. Marshall stayed with the 5th New York until the Battle of Antietam in September 1862. On the advice of Colonel Warren, Marshall left for safe haven in Alexandria to avoid the possibility of capture during the battle or in the event of a Union retreat. Once in Alexandria, Marshall found employment and shelter in the government stables.[9]

The absence of slave owners and overseers also provided the right circumstances for self-emancipation. Richard Dixon was a slave on the Stringfellow Farm in Faquier County, Virginia. Dixon's owner, Howard Stringfellow, fled at the approach of the Union Army and before leaving asked the slaves to look after the crops and property. In the planter's absence, Dixon and his family moved to Washington in January 1863.[10]

Though military events provided the safest opportunities for escape, many slaves eluded the bonds of human ownership from border state slave masters; some even escaped through the Confederate lines. For example, George H. Boston, who was raised on a plantation in Alabama, ran away from a plantation in Charles County, Maryland, only a week before he joined the army. The hazards erected by slave owners to discourage fugitive slaves—such as mounted patrols and threats of severe punishments—made Boston's escape to Washington a dangerous undertaking.[11] George Coombs, an enslaved farm laborer from LaPlata, Maryland, made the hazardous trip to Washington in August 1862. Coombs left his family on the farm, changed his surname to Brent, and found employment at Columbia Hospital as a "government hand" at the pay of ten dollars a month.[12] In 1862, Welcome Lee, a slave laborer from Elizabeth City, North Carolina, escaped to Roanoke Island, where he worked with the Union quartermaster corps building fortifications. From Roanoke Island, Lee went first to New Berne, North Carolina, and then to Alexandria, Virginia, as a government laborer.[13] Armstead Bond, a slave laborer from Norfolk County, Virginia, escaped to Suffolk, Virginia, in the fall of 1862. Prior to his escape, Bond drove a Confederate forage wagon. Upon arriving at Suffolk, Bond traveled with a group of contrabands to Norfolk city to work as government laborers. He later worked in Alexandria and then Washington as a cook.[14]

The Emancipation Proclamation, more so than previous legislation, contributed to Washington's status as a place of safety. Lincoln's proclamation freed slaves in the rebellious states while respecting slave owners' rights in the border states. This, in effect, inspired slaves to leave Confederate-held areas and border states in increasing numbers. As a result, fugitive slaves from neighboring Virginia and Maryland came to view Washington as an oasis of hope. Enslaved Virginians escaped to Washington to realize the freedom promised in the Emancipation Proclamation, while Maryland slaves sought refuge and anonymity in Washington's large black population.

By mid-1863, the African American population of Washington contained a wide variety of people representing different aspects of antebellum black America. Though living conditions for African Americans ranged from poor to fair, the prospect of freedom and the intimation of social autonomy more than outweighed the possibility of capture, poverty, or death from disease and exposure. The revolutionary acts of Congress and the president imbued many black Washingtonians, natives and immigrants, with a greater sense of hope and patriotism. From this mixed population of freed and free men came the volunteers for the 1st United States Colored Infantry.

Besides providing a greater impetus for slaves to escape, the Emancipation Proclamation offered black men the opportunity to fight for freedom. The proclamation authorized the enlistment of black men into the army as garrison troops and aboard all vessels of the navy. As a result, African Americans and abolitionists throughout the free states and occupied South began petitioning the government for permission to raise black regiments, as did governors of several Northern states. In the District of Columbia, the Reverend J. D. Turner (an abolitionist and former chaplain of the Fourth Pennsylvania Cavalry) and 67 "prominent" black Washingtonians petitioned the War Department in January 1863 for the authority to raise a regiment. Their request was granted in April.[15]

On May 4, Turner began recruitment of the 1st District of Columbia Colored Volunteer Infantry at the contraband camp on 12th and E streets. Thirty contrabands enlisted. That evening, Turner held a "war meeting" at the Asbury Methodist Church. He began with a stirring patriotic speech, followed by addresses from prominent black civic leaders and clergy. During the speeches recruiting agents stalked the isles and took the names of potential recruits. As a precaution against trouble, members of the 39th Massachusetts Cavalry guarded the doors. Many of Washington's black churches held similar war meetings to aid recruiting efforts.[16]

In the latter part of May 1863 the Federal government created the Bureau of Colored Troops as a means of managing the recruitment, officer selection, and administration of the colored regiments. Under the direction of Colonel William Birney, who headed recruitment of USCTs in the departments of Washington and Maryland, civilian recruiting continued unabated. Appropriately, the 1st District of Columbia became the first regiment raised under the auspices of the Bureau of Colored Troops and was, therefore, re-designated the 1st United States Colored Infantry (U.S.C.I.). Due to a lack of training facilities, the recruits initially were housed in the contraband camp, as well as in private homes and black churches. On May 21, 1863, the Bureau of Colored Troops moved the

Chaplain Henry McNeal Turner, a minister in the African Methodist Episcopal church, was the first black chaplain commissioned in the United States Colored Troops. Turner was elected to the Georgia legislature in 1867, and became a bishop in the AME church in 1880. Disillusioned with the failure of Reconstruction, he became an advocate of black nationalism and seperation of the races.

Moorland-Springarn Research Center, Howard University

volunteers to "Camp Green" on Mason's Island in the Potomac River, and
placed them under the command of Colonel John Holman. Camp Green offered
the volunteers a military setting ideal for training purposes and protection from
the possible abuses of Southern sympathizers.[17]

George Boston's transition from civilian to solder is typical. Boston enlisted
under Colonel Birney at "Sadies Hall" near the Capitol grounds, and then he and
a few other recruit were temporarily billeted in a private home on the corner of
1st and B streets for nearly a month before moving to Mason's Island. Upon
their arrival at Camp Green, Boston and 25 other recruits stripped and received
medical examinations. Those who were found physically fit took an oath and
received uniforms and equipment. George Hatton also enlisted at Sadies Hall
and went to Mason's Island, but unlike Boston, he mustered into the regiment as
a sergeant. Charles Gurtrige signed-up at Mason's Island and remembered receiving a dress coat, fatigue blouse, overcoat, cap, a pair of shoes, two pairs of
socks, a pair of drawers, two shirts, a wool blanket, a rubber blanket, a knap-
sack, haversack, canteen, and a dinner setting for one person. Because the
government planned to use black soldiers primarily as fatigue troops, Gurtrige
was issued an old smooth bore Harper's Ferry musket instead of a newer model
rifle. When Armstead Bond enlisted, Colonel Birney requested Bond's father's
name and advised Bond to use it instead of his former owner's name. Recruiters
promised the 1st U.S.C.I. volunteers $13 monthly pay and a $50 enlistment
bonus.[18]

Though the recruiting of the 1st U.S.C.I. went relatively smoothly, angry
white citizens and the apprehensions of potential volunteers posed a few significant problems. Many white Washingtonians resented the repeal of the Black
Codes, the presence of contrabands, and the actions of Radical Republicans on
Capitol Hill. The recruitment of a black regiment in Washington represented
another imposition of the Republican administration. Some of the more resentful
citizens even attacked the black recruits. When a mob attacked Cpl. John Ross
after a war meeting on June 1, 1863, a metropolitan police officer intervened
and dispersed the mob, but he also repeatedly clubbed the corporal. Military
officials later arrested the police officer for abusing a United States soldier. The
hostile actions of a few hateful citizens thus proved an irritant to recruiting
efforts but failed to dampen the hopes and spirits of patriotic volunteers. When
for example, a drunken white soldier shouted at a black recruit to "get out of the
road you damned nigger," the proud recruit replied, "look at what you say . . .
[you] can't call me a nigger no more."[19]

The transformation from civilian to soldier brought to the recruits a sense of self-respect, optimism, and freedom. The uniform imbued them with federal authority, prestige, and a claim to citizenship. By enlisting, the volunteers had taken the first step toward liberating their brethren and uplifting their race. Despite a few mishaps, the 1st U.S.C.I. had a relatively peaceful stay on Mason's Island. On August 3, 1863, the regiment left Camp Green to start its tour of duty in the Department of Virginia and North Carolina.[20]

The excitement of adventure and visions of glory usually accompanied the movement of troops to the front. For the men of the 1st U.S.C.I., two major disappointments marred their transfer to the seat of war in the summer of 1863. The first was the War Department's decision to pay black troops, regardless of rank, $10 per month and deduct $3 per month for clothing, which starkly contradicted the earlier promises of $13 per month plus a clothing allowance (the same as white soldiers). War Department officials justified their decision on the provisions of the 1862 Militia Act, which authorized the express use of blacks as military laborers at a wage of $10 per month. The second disappointment came when the troops set aside their antiquated muskets for picks and shovels. The regiment's initial duties in Virginia and North Carolina consisted of building fortifications and defenses for white troops. Though these discriminatory acts remained major issues throughout most of the war, the men served honorably while seeking justice.[21]

Transported on a leaky troop ship to Fort Monroe, Virginia, the 1st U.S.C.I. transferred to safer transports and steamed for New Berne, North Carolina. The regiment stayed in New Berne for one night and embarked for Plymouth, North Carolina the next day. After its arrival the regiment settled into a routine of garrison and fatigue duty. The hard work and daily routine of constructing breastworks and manning defenses gave the soldiers some time to mull over the pay difference. Sergeant John R. Tunnia wrote to the Philadelphia *Christian Recorder* regarding the men's anger over pay: "we don't feel like serving . . . under such an imposition; we were promised $13 per month and a bounty." The soldiers' frustrations became more acute with time and service. The regiment stayed at Plymouth a month before shipping off to Portsmouth, Virginia to go into winter quarters.[22]

On November 10, 1863, the 1st U.S.C.I. and the 1st and 2nd North Carolina Colored Volunteers were assigned to the command of Brig. Gen. Edward A. Wild and designated Wild's African Brigade (1st Brigade, 3rd Division, Army of the James). The fatigue work continued, but not for long.[23] On December 5, 1863, Maj. Gen. Benjamin Butler, commander of the Army of the James, ordered

General Wild to lead an expedition into the northeastern counties of North Carolina for the purpose of restoring Union control over the Dismal Swamp Canal, aiding Unionist residents, dispersing Rebel guerrillas, and procuring recruits.[24] The expedition, described as a raid by members of the 1st U.S.C.I., was a cold, wet, and miserable experience. The brigade took a route through the Dismal Swamp that paralleled the canal. Sergeant Theodore Ray became very ill after marching 31 miles in "ugly and cold" weather without shoes. Apparently Ray had slept too close to a campfire and ruined his only pair of boots. Adverse weather conditions and exposure disabled several other men. Private John Brown, for example, contracted "chills and fever" and later testified to a pension commissioner that exposure to the weather caused neuralgia and rheumatism in his left leg.[25]

While on the march to Elizabeth City, an incident worthy of mention occurred in South Mills. Colonel Holman arrested John W. Hinton, a prominent slave owner, for sending two enslaved children across enemy lines. The children, Mary and Oscar Williams, were the offspring of Pvt. George Williams. Holman ordered Hinton, the uncle of a local Confederate colonel, to remain in custody until Private Williams' children were returned. Though regimental records do not reveal the outcome of Hinton's arrest, this incident highlights Holman's commitment to his regiment and its members, and their struggle against slavery.[26]

Upon reaching Elizabeth City, the 1st U.S.C.I. attempted to restore Union control through patrols and guard posts. Based upon reports that Confederate guerrillas were shooting unarmed men and burning the houses of Unionists, Holman instituted a 9:30 p.m. curfew and prohibited the assembly of three or more persons for political purposes. John Haynes remembered serving picket duty "on a dark and rainy night . . .[when]. . . intelligence was brought" to his regiment that John Wilcox, a Southern spy, had collected provisions to smuggle behind Confederate lines. A squad of pickets promptly arrested Wilcox at his residence. While running to Wilcox's house, Haynes became the regiment's only casualty in this action after he fell into a post hole and severely injured his right leg. Otherwise, the "raid" was a success; General Wild reported that the brigade burned four guerrilla camps, confiscated 50 guns and a cache of ammunition, and liberated 2,500 slaves.[27]

For the men of the 1st U.S.C.I., the raid represented their first opportunity to fill the role of liberators. Their presence greatly aided the restoration of Federal authority in Elizabeth City and, more importantly, brought freedom to a significant number of their enslaved brethren. In essence, the raid allowed the men to actualize their reasons for enlisting and savor the fruits of victory.

When the 1st U.S.C.I. returned to Portsmouth in mid-December 1863, the rigors and tedium of garrison and fatigue duty also returned. Assignment to special details helped alleviate the monotony. In January 1864, division head-quarters in Portsmouth chose the 1st U.S.C.I. to act as a provost guard, an honor usually extended to highly-rated white regiments. This assignment represented progress and prestige for the soldiers. Colonel Holman commended the men on their military bearing and ability to overcome racial barriers to "receive the commendation of the commanding general." In addition to this regimental-level assignment, individual soldiers were picked from each company and detailed as clerks, carpenters, and blacksmiths attached to the brigade or division headquar-ters, and as sharpshooters, teamsters, and hospital stewards with division or corps headquarters. These details reflected a significant level of literacy and skill in the ranks, and allowed a vacation from the pick-axe and shovel as well as a wel-comed change of routine.[28]

The monotony and heavy labor of garrison and fatigue duty only served to increase tensions over unequal pay. The troops had worked and served faithfully and expected fair treatment. Moreover, the difference of $3 meant much to the impoverished families of soldiers. First Sergeant Lincoln Lewis noted on Febru-ary 1, 1864, that Pvt. William Jones "shot [his] fingers off right hand" in discon-solation over the pay issue and as a means of getting discharged. On February 8, Lewis noted that the "small pay makes regiment dispirited." When the regiment moved to New Berne, North Carolina, in February, unequal pay remained a pressing issue. Sergeant George Hatton expressed his humiliation in a letter to the *Christian Recorder*. Hatton wondered "why the United States hesitates in giving us our full pay. Have we not proved ourselves as soldiers?" He further asked, "did we not come forward to assist in protecting her [the United States] without meditating for a moment on . . . how our fore-fathers and mothers had been treated. . . ?" Though frustrated, Hatton reaffirmed his reason for serving by stating that "we are too patriotic to our race not to distinguish ourselves when the opportunity is offered." The pay issue was just another obstacle to overcome in the fight for full citizenship.[29]

On February 12, 1864, the regiment was ordered back to New Bern to prepare defenses for an expected spring attack. First Sergeant Lewis noted in the morning report of March 3 that "every available officer and man began working on trenches and building rifle pits." On March 4, he wrote that his company built a five-embrasure battery with abatis. The regiment also drilled to maintain a high state of combat readiness. Yet the expectation of battle also led many of the men to seek security in their religious beliefs. First Sergeant Samuel Allen wrote, "I will fight as long as a slave can be seen, and if it is my lot to be cut down in battle. . .I shall be saved." Allen also recounted a song the soldiers sang: "We are the Gallant First, who slightly have been tried; when ordered into battle, take Jesus for our guide." Fortunately for the men of the 1st U.S.C.I., who were still armed with antiquated smoothbores, Confederate forces attacked and captured Plymouth instead of New Berne. On April 25, the regiment boarded the steamer *Webster* for their return to Fort Monroe.[30]

The troops arrived at Fort Monroe on April 27, 1864, where they received modern Enfield rifled-muskets and departed for Camp Hamilton near City Point, Virginia. At City Point, the regiment joined approximately 40,000 other black troops in the Army of the James. They were amassed by General Butler for possible offensive operations near Richmond. Sergeant Hatton stood in awe at the sight of so many black soldiers. "Though I have been a soldier for more than a year," he remarked, "I had never witnessed such a sight before . . . so you may imagine my feelings at finding myself attached to an Army of my own color." Hatton concluded that "I felt as though I were in some other country where slavery was never known." On April 28, the 1st U.S.C.I. moved to Wilson's Wharf, near Jamestown, and began building fortifications in preparation for the 1864 campaign season.[31]

The proximity of Wilson's Wharf to Jamestown, the first port of entry for African slaves in British North America, was not lost on the men of the 1st U.S.C.I., a number of whom were natives of the area. In a May 10 letter to the *Christian Recorder*, Sergeant Hatton described an incident that made the connection between the location and the armed struggle for equality much more significant. A foraging party from the regiment captured a notorious planter named Clapton, who earlier had severely beaten several female slaves. Colonel Holman had Clapton tied to a tree and whipped by the women and Pvt. William Harris, who at one time also had been a slave on Clapton's farm. Hatton could barely articulate his emotions. "[O]h, that I had the tongue to express my feelings while standing upon the James [R]iver on the soil of Virginia, the mother state of slavery, as a witness of such a sudden reverse," he wrote. Hatton saw the incident as testimony to the belief that finally "colored men have ascended upon a platform of equality."[32]

While the black soldiers built fortifications and meted out retribution, Confederate forces took the offensive. The regiment's seminal trial in battle occurred at Wilson's Wharf only "a few miles from the very spot where the first sons of

Africa were landed," one of the black soldiers later wrote. Chaplain Henry M. Turner recalled that the Confederate attack occurred around noon on May 24, while he was coming back from his dinner. Many of the men were eating when the long roll—the call to arms—was sounded. According to Turner, "It required only a few moments to find every man, sick or well, drawn into line of battle" while two companies skirmished with dismounted Confederate cavalry. After a brief engagement, Confederate Gen. Fitzhugh Lee, with a force of approximately 3,000 men and three cannon, called a truce to request the surrender of the outnumbered Union garrison. General Wild declined Lee's offer and instead ordered an attack on the Confederates. With the aid of a navy gunboat, the 1st. U.S.C.I. assaulted and repelled Lee's force. The black regiment suffered a loss of two killed and 19 wounded, while inflicting 24 killed, six wounded, and four captured from the Confederate ranks. Chaplain Turner overstated the results of the battle when he boasted that the 1st U.S.C.I. "unmercifully slaughtered" the Confederates. He was a bit more realistic when he wrote that the Confederates "fled before our men, carrying a large number of their dead." There was a more significant message here, one that Turner used as a means of addressing the pay issue. The chaplain was quick to note that the white artillerymen who witnessed the battle "think it is a burning shame for the government to keep these men [of the 1st U.S.C.I.] out of their full pay."[33]

In June 1864, the 1st U.S.C.I. joined Ulysses S. Grant's forces around Petersburg for the opening of the siege which would eventually encompass nine long months. On June 14, Union forces under Gen. William F. "Baldy" Smith approached Petersburg from the rear for a surprise attack. The next day, General Edward W. Hincks' "Colored Division," which included the 1st U.S.C.I., charged the defenses of the city. The 22nd U.S.C.I. from Philadelphia, the 4th U.S.C.I. from Baltimore, and the 5th U.S.C.I. from Ohio led the attack, while the 1st U.S.C.I. was in reserve. The Colored Division took the first line of defenses at 9:00 a.m. and waited until 5:00 p.m. to resume the attack. At 6:00, the 1st U.S.C.I. led the second advance and carried the second line of defenses.[34]

The delay between attacks allowed the reinforcement of Confederate forces, which rendered impractical the idea of a third attack. Chaplain Turner remembered arriving in the 1st U.S.C.I.'s camp on June 15 only to find it empty. He and the chaplain of the 4th U.S.C.I. rode toward the sound of musket fire. They arrived on the battlefield in time to see the first set of attackers capture two Confederate batteries. Turner exclaimed that the black troops "flayed the scoundrels as they would a set of mad dogs." Turner joined the skirmishers from the his own regiment while the other troops waited for the order to make a second attack.

He recalled that "the troops lay under the galling fire of the rebel forts and sharpshooters for nearly eight hours. . .[and that] the only chance a man had for his life was to lie flat . . . ." In spite of this, Turner wrote, "a shell would often burst in the ranks and sever arms and legs from bodies."[35]

When the second attack was finally ordered, the 1st U.S.C.I. charged the second line of Confederate defenses, screaming "Fort Pillow!" while they ran, in reference to the slaughter of black soldiers by Nathan Bedford Forrest's troops earlier in the year. To carry the enemy works, the regiment had to cross ditches, traverse ravines, and surmount abatis. A number of troops received injuries charging over this rough ground. Private George Boston, for instance, broke two ribs when he slipped and fell against a log abatis, and Pvt. Baylor Bromley suffered serious head injuries from a limb felled by cannon fire. Once inside the Confederate defenses, Turner saw the Southerners fleeing and Union troops shooting Confederate prisoners, a heinous act that nevertheless "was highly endorsed by a number of both white and colored." This victory cost the 1st U.S.C.I. 17 killed, 114 wounded, and 25 missing.[36]

After the post-battle elation diminished, the 1st U.S.C.I. again faced issues of inequality. Wounded during the battle, Sergeant Hatton became furious when military officials denied his father's request to take him home as a convalescent, a privilege allowed white parents. Hatton wrote: "All of this I was willing to stand . . . I was wounded for the low United States' degrading sum of $7 per month, that no man but . . . the patriotic black man would be willing to fight for." While recounting the battle for the *Christian Recorder*, a private of Company K posed a rhetorical question concerning the issue of unequal pay and citizenship. He wondered why, "after doing such daring exploits, we do not deserve the rights and privileges of the United States of America? Are we to fight for the dastardly sum of seven dollars a month, while our wives and children are starving at home?" Though frustrated with the existing injustices, the men gained a stronger sense of confidence and pride after the battle. They sang "we are the gallant First, who noble—have been tried—ready and willing, with our bayonets by our side."[37]

The failure of Union forces to capture Petersburg, and thus Richmond, forced General Grant to lay siege to the cities. During the siege, which lasted from June 16, 1864, to April 3, 1865, the 1st U.S.C.I. participated in two attempts to break the Confederate defenses. The first, at the Battle of Fort Harrison, occurred on September 29, 1864. The attack on Fort Harrison was part of a larger plan aimed at reducing the defenses of Richmond and was correlated with attacks on New Market Heights and Fort Gilmer, collectively known as the

Battle of Chaffin's Farm. During the attack on Fort Harrison, the 1st U.S.C.I. remained in reserve and did not go into battle. The regiment's casualties resulted from a bombardment of its position and the use of a few of its troops as sharpshooters and skirmishers. Private James Robert, for instance, lost an arm to a solid shot while he stood in reserve; a shell fragment broke Pvt. Richard Parker's right leg; and Pvt. Edward Carter received a wound to the right leg while deployed as a skirmisher with the sharpshooters. After Union forces captured Fort Harrison, they had to endure a two-day bombardment and counterattack during which the 1st U.S.C.I. also suffered additional casualties. Sergeant James Adams and another soldier received leg injuries during an intense bombardment which drove the entire Union garrison into the fort. The regiment lost three killed and 18 wounded in the Harrison fight.[38]

The second major battle involving the 1st U.S.C.I. occurred on October 27, 1864, at Fair Oaks, Virginia. The regiment was ordered to threaten the Confederate left flank to divert attention from the main effort against the right flank. The main assault became confused and disjointed, allowing the Confederate forces to concentrate their strength against the diversion. In response, the 1st U.S.C.I., supported by the 22nd U.S.C.I., charged the enemy positions and captured two guns. The sheer number of Confederate troops forced the black soldiers to abandon the captured pieces and ground and withdraw to the safety of Union gun emplacements. The gallant actions of men such as Pvt. John Minus, Colonel Holman, and Capt. Henry Ward garnered the regiment much praise. Private Minus charged into the enemy's defenses and engaged in hand-to-hand combat until disabled by a blow to the back with a musket butt. Colonel Holman charged at the head of the regiment until he received a gunshot wound to the thigh, and Captain Ward was taken prisoner when he stayed behind to spike two Confederate cannon. The performance of the 1st U.S.C.I. at the Battle of Fair Oaks led Thomas Morris Chester, a black war correspondent, to comment that "the 1st U.S.C.I. is a fighting regiment . . . they have never been known to falter." At Fair Oaks, the regiment lost 12 killed, 96 wounded, and 16 missing and assumed captured.[39]

The regiment performed fatigue and picket duty during much of its sojourn around Petersburg. The circumstances, however, proved to be very dangerous, Turner recalled, for the Union pickets offered good targets for Confederate sharpshooters. Corporal Richard Parker, for instance, received a gunshot wound that fractured his left arm while he was on picket duty. The regiment's position, which was nearly opposite Confederate Fort Clifton, provided the Southerners with a plethora of soldiers to shoot at. Besides picket duty, members of the regiment regularly worked on fatigue details in the trenches, shoring up defenses, or at Dutch Gap excavating a canal within the range of Confederate batteries. Turner stated that "the workmen are constantly harassed by the explosion of rebel shells" and that "our pickets and the . . . the rebels are within talking distance." In a pension claim for a shell wound that Sgt. Joseph Taylor received while in charge of a work detail at Dutch Gap, First Lt. Nicholas Larney corroborated Turner's account when he testified that the working parties were continually under the enemy's fire.[40]

As a means of finding solace from the hazards and monotony of duty near Petersburg, the men wrote letters, read, learned to read, and attended prayer meetings. In a July 16 article in the *Christian Recorder*, Turner asked families and friends to write the troops because "he [the soldier] might possibly write a few words, he is so exhausted . . . he falls to sleep, and when he wakes some thief has stolen his paper, ink and pen, or it has rained and destroyed his paper." In an October 8 article, Turner informed *Recorder* readers that "we have preaching three times every Sabbath, and most of the remaining intervals are consumed in prayer meetings." He also related that spelling books were in high demand throughout the regiment, since many of the illiterate men grew tired and ashamed of having someone read to them and wanted to become literate. Furthermore, the weekly packages of *Recorders* and *Anglo-Africans* did not satiate the demand for reading materials. In an article written on November 28, Turner stated that the men, through the improvement of their reading skills, "are trying to prepare for whatever position the future may offer," a testament to the soldiers' expectations of full citizenship after the war.[41]

On December 8, 1864, the 1st U.S.C.I. received a break from the routine of siege duty when it joined the first expedition against Fort Fisher, North Carolina. This fort served as the Confederate stronghold that guarded the entrance to the Cape Fear River and assured the safe passage of the blockade runners that supplied Lee's army. Major General Benjamin Butler hoped to destroy the fort by loading a ship with 215 tons of gunpower and detonating it near the fort's ocean face. His 6,500 men, it was naively assumed, would simply walk in and capture the stunned garrison. Chaplain Turner provided a daily report of events to the *Christian Recorder*. The 1st and 37th U.S.C.I. boarded the transport *Herman Livingston* on the night of December 8. The transport, part of the largest fleet assembled during the war, sailed for Washington in an attempt to confuse the Confederates. Once out of sight, the ship made way for Cape Hatteras, N. C., and arrived six days later. Several severe storms made the water so rough, however, that Butler postponed the attack. On Christmas Eve, Union sailors ignited the gunpowder-filled vessel. The tremendous explosion rattled windows miles away and created a spectacular pyrotechnics display—but did not cause any damage to Fort Fisher. The next day, December 25, Butler bombarded the fort and attempted an assault. But the troops, who captured a few guns and Confederate soldiers on the beach, withdrew after Butler became apprehensive of the fort's strong appearance. Only a few men of the 1st U.S.C.I. saw any action or even left the transports. Those who fought at Fort Fisher served with a sharp-shooter company which skirmished across the Cape Fear River. The regiment's casualties resulted from shipboard accidents and sea sickness. Private David Livers, for example, fell through a hatchway while storing his musket and se-verely injured his side. Chaplain Turner joyfully noted that the regiment set sail for Fortress Monroe on December 27 and arrived on the 28th. "We received orders to proceed up the James river to our old quarters, which we did more than willingly," he wrote.[42]

The regiment had barely settled back into camp when it received orders on January 3, 1865, to proceed to Bermuda Landing for the second Fort Fisher Expedition. In frustration over Butler's failed effort, Lincoln and Grant decided to replace Butler with Maj. Gen. Alfred H. Terry and launch a second attempt. The transports sailed on January 4 and arrived off Fort Fisher eight days later. The next day, January 13, the 1st U.S.C.I.—as part of the Third Brigade, Third Division, of the mostly black XXV Army Corps—disembarked two and a half miles above the fort and began constructing a line of entrenchments across the Cape Fear peninsula facing Wilmington. Its mission was to hold that line while other Union forces stormed the fort, thereby preventing the escape of the bas-tion's garrison or reinforcement from Confederate forces entrenched several miles to the north on the Sugar Loaf line.[43]

On January 13, the Union navy opened a barrage that rained 800 tons of munitions on Fort Fisher and its garrison. Two days later, with most of the fort's guns disabled, 4,500 soldiers and 2,000 marines and sailors made an amphibious assault which captured the fort after a few hours of hard fighting. After the fort's surrender, the 1st U.S.C.I., with the rest Brig. Gen. Charles J. Paine's third division, made camp and set about performing garrison duties in and about the captured stronghold.[44]

On February 11, General Paine received orders to advance toward Sugar Loaf Hill, just below Wilmington. Upon encountering entrenched enemy pickets, Paine deployed the 4th U.S.C.I as skirmishers. After a brief fight, the pickets retreated into the main works and the division settled into a line of trenches in front of Sugar Loaf. On February 19, Paine received word that the Southern troops had evacuated Sugar Loaf and were retreating towards Wilmington. In accordance with orders from Major General Terry, the Third division—with the 1st U.S.C.I in the lead—broke camp and marched in pursuit. After skirmishing with the Confederate rear guard on the morning of February 20, the men found their adversaries entrenched in earthworks about five miles below Wilmington. Paine advanced the Third Brigade and deployed the 5th U.S.C.I as skirmishers. Ironically, the 1st U.S.C.I was held in reserve during the ensuing fight and yet suffered its only battle fatality of the campaign when a Confederate shell killed Pvt. Peter Lee of Company F. After a brief skirmish, the division entrenched and waited. On the morning of February 22, a delighted Paine found the Confederate works empty and the road to Wilmington clear. At 9:00 a.m., the Third Division entered the long-sought city unopposed.[45]

After a brief rest, General Terry ordered Paine to pursue the retreating Confederates. From February 22 to March 24, Paine's division skirmished continuously through much of North Carolina. By March 21st, Union forces had reached Cox's Bridge on the Neuse River, where the First, Fifth, and Tenth U.S.C.I. repulsed a vigorous attack, after which they marched to Faison's Depot on the Wilmington and Weldon Railroad to rest and recuperate.[46]

To many members of the 1st U.S.C.I., the expedition in North Carolina tested their endurance. Though the regiment suffered only one killed and 11 wounded during the campaign, it suffered numerous other casualties from exposure and exhaustion. Sergeant Tunnia found "the roads were very wet, sand was very heavy, and a great many streams to cross." He described the campaign as "a series of long hard marches" in which many men suffered with colds and rheumatism. Sgt. James Adams characterized the experience as "a sort of running fight across the Neuse river clear up to Wilmington."[47]

In contrast, Chaplain Turner described the campaign as a light-hearted affair filled with food and frolic. In the April 15, 1865, issue of the *Christian Recorder*, Turner stated that forage was plentiful and that many of the soldiers gathered the livestock and produce of Southern farmers. He recalled an instance when he pulled some fodder from a hay stack for his horse and uncovered a cache of hams, smoked pork shoulders, and several sides of bacon, all of which he gladly liberated. Although foraging generally deprived the inhabitants of much needed sustenance, Turner reported that black soldiers, in contrast to their vengeful white comrades, always left some food for the white women and children. According to Turner, the black troops acted as victors and liberators while their white counterparts sought to punish Southerners for starting a bloody and protracted war. Turner also recounted the crossing of streams in jovial prose.

"Some [soldiers] would simply hang their cartridge boxes on their bayonets and plunge in with a cheerful yell . . . others would strip naked with their clothes [lifted] over their heads," and "like some monstrous brood of liberated ducks take to the water." He also observed soldiers attacking domestic bee hives with bayonets to get the honey, leaving the angry bees to seek revenge on soldiers in the rear columns. No doubt, Turner's account reflected his involvement from horseback instead of on foot.[48]

The transformation from an oppressed group of black soldiers to the role of conquerors became readily apparent during the campaign when they came in contact with ardent Confederate sympathizers. One particular incident involved a planter who, upon the approach of the 1st U.S.C.I., released a slave woman from irons. Upon hearing about the planter's cruelty, the regiment wrecked his "splendid mansion." As Turner described the scene, when the planter spoke "saucily" to one of the men, "he was sent headlong to the floor by a blow across the mouth, his downward tendency being materially accelerated by an application of boot leather." The black troops personified Federal authority and as such demanded respect for themselves and the liberated slaves. Later that evening, white soldiers, many of whom had served and suffered for four years under the hardships of war, burned the planter's house to the ground.[49]

After the Confederate surrender on April 26 at the Bennett House near Durham, the 1st U.S.C.I. served as occupation troops in the newly-created Department of North Carolina. The regiment's duties included assisting freedmen in the transition from slavery, imposing Federal authority on the population, and maintaining civil order. Chaplain Turner noted that ex-Confederates abused freedmen and, in some instances, had managed to return former slaves to a state of servitude. Ironically, white Union soldiers created the first disturbance in which the 1st U.S.C.I. directly intervened on behalf of the freedmen. The incident began when a group of white soldiers began cursing freedmen. A group of black soldiers arrived on the scene and "returned the compliment," which incited a fist fight. The altercation ended when guards from the 1st U.S.C.I. arrested the instigators. The Union victory and expectations of going home eroded the anti-Southern attitudes of some whites. Furthermore, the vulnerable state of the freedmen, coupled with shared notions of white supremacy, lessened the tensions between white Union soldiers and ex-Confederates. Turner complained that it was common for white soldiers to curse, threaten, and whip freedmen to "gratify some secesh belle or to keep the good will of some Southerner who can keep a sumptuous table." Nonetheless, a few white residents, according to Turner, preferred the presence of black troops because white soldiers were "troublesome to their wives and daughters."[50]

The paucity of food and other vital supplies posed a threat to the Southern population. Turner reported that thousands of whites traveled long distances to draw government rations, but many residents, black and white, still died of starvation. For the hungry of both races, the 1st U.S.C.I. and other black regiments represented hope and salvation. Invariably, the prospect of death humbled white Southerners and reinforced the role of black troops as conquerors. Turner recalled that "several white ladies and slave oligarchs" entered his office to request rations "in the same humiliating custom which they formerly would have expected from me." It greatly satisfied Turner "to see them crouching before me, and I a negro."[51]

The presence of black occupation troops emboldened the former bondsmen to relinquish the slave persona and live as free citizens. The confidence and independence that black soldiers exhibited set an example for the freedmen. Turner, for instance, stated that the troops carried themselves like "magic lords, swaggering on in their exultant conquest." The effect on black civilians was revolutionary. One former slave and his son-in-law went as far as to arrest a Confederate veteran who had threatened them. The two men disarmed their assailant, restrained him with rope, and marched him 10 miles to the 1st U.S.C.I.'s headquarters. Though extreme, this incident exemplified the courage and dignity that freedmen acquired while under the protection of black troops.[52]

On June 3, the regiment moved its headquarters to Roanoke Island. There Colonel Holman discovered that the contraband laborers were starving due to the graft of government agents, some of whom Holman placed under arrest. The agents had issued government laborers worthless I.O.U.s and pocketed the freedmen's money and rations. Still, Chaplain Turner reported that those freedmen who had received one-acre land allotments lived in suitable homes with "excellent gardens," and that they produced an abundance of eggs and poultry— a testament to the success of land ownership over wage labor. Unfortunately, government agents and the Freedman's Bureau opted for the latter and indirectly aided planters in their efforts to deny the freedmen the former.[53]

The discharge of many white regiments and the lack of adequate numbers of troops to garrison the entire region left freedmen open to the abuses of returning Confederate soldiers. Holman complained that former Confederates had threatened the lives of a party of blacks he had sent to Elizabeth City for employment. Furthermore, Holman wrote, "two gross outrages were committed upon unoffending colored women" in Elizabeth City. Holman resolved that "it would be inhuman to send them [freedmen] there to be simply murdered by returned rebels and worthless vagabonds." In two other incidents involving the abuse of freedmen, Holman threatened to use force as a solution. He stated that many ex-Confederates were not "likely to show much regard for the law until some of them feel its power." Though the 1st U.S.C.I. lacked the manpower to meet all emergencies, Chaplain Turner noted that the mere presence of black troops curbed wanton abuse and violence against black civilians. The threat of force and the willingness of members of the regiment to defend the freed population deterred flagrant abuses in their jurisdiction.[54]

The 1st U.S.C.I.'s occupation duty in North Carolina was a unique and enlightening experience for many of the regiment's members. During their brief stay, they served as the civil authority and addressed humanitarian concerns. Former slave owners as well as poor yeomen farmers sought food and clothing from the black soldiers. For once, black men formed a dominant and powerful force. According to Turner, returning Confederate soldiers seemed "to be musing as to whether they are actually in another world or whether this one is turned wrong side out." The experience instilled in the 1st U.S.C.I. veterans a new self-assuredness and sense of social equality. Most of the soldiers would never again realize the same levels of freedom and authority they enjoyed as conquerors, liberators, and humanitarians.[55]

The 1st United States Colored Infantry mustered out of Federal service on September 29, 1865, at Roanoke Island, North Carolina, and prepared for the return trip to Washington, D. C. During the war, the regiment lost five officers and 180 enlisted men killed in action or dead from wounds and disease, and many more were discharged because of wounds and sickness. The regiment arrived in Washington on October 8 at the Seventh Street wharf to the cheers of black Washingtonians. The *Evening Star* reported that "thousands of colored people" escorted the regiment to Campbell Military Hospital, which stood on the present site of Howard University. That evening, the veterans encamped on the hospital grounds and became reunited with family and friends.[56]

For the soldiers of the 1st United States Colored Infantry, the war was over, but the struggle for their civil rights was just beginning.

Notes

1. Frederick Dyer, *A Compendium of the War of the Rebellion*, vol. III (New York: 1956), 1,723; Regimental Books and Papers, 1st United States Colored Infantry, Record

Group (hereinafter RG) 94: Record of the Adjutant General's Office, National Archives, Washington, D.C. (hereinafter NA).

2. Constance M. Green, *The Secret City: A History of Race Relations in the Nation's Capital* (Princeton, New Jersey: 1967), 172-84; Margaret Leech, *Reveille in Washington: 1860-1865* (New York: 1941), 236-41.

3. Ibid., 35-54; Ira Berlin, et. al., eds. *Freedom: A Documentary History of Emancipation, 1861-1867*, ser. I, vol. I, *The Destruction of Slavery* (Cambridge: 1985), 5, 159.

4. Green, Secret City, 47-54; Deposition of Charles Gurtrige, March 8, 1889, Pension Files of Charles Gurtrige, RG15, NA; Deposition of George W. Hatton, December 26, 1900, Pension File of George W. Hatton, RG 15, NA; Deposition of Richard Henderson, December 19, 1900, Pension File of Richard Henderson, RG 15, NA.

5. Barbara Jeanne Fields, *Slavery and Freedom on the Middle Ground: Maryland during the Nineteenth Century* (New Haven: 1985), 117-19; Berlin, *The Destruction of Slavery*, 11-16, 160-63, 331-34. Fugitive slaves and a number of free blacks from Virginia sought asylum from impressment into the Confederate labor gangs. Confederate slave laborers generally worked on fortifications.

6. James M. McPherson, *Battle Cry of Freedom: The Civil War Era* (New York: 1989), 354-58; Berlin, *Destruction of Slavery*, 14-20; Ira Berlin, et. al., eds., *Free at Last: A Documentary History of Slavery, Freedom, and The Civil War* (New York: 1992), 167-213. It is important to note that General Butler and the First Confiscation Act excluded the slaves of owners living in the loyal border states. Loyal Marylanders, for example, had a right to claim fugitives slaves.

7. Green, *The Secret City*, 55-66; Leech, *Reveille in Washington*, 236-24; Regimental Descriptive Books and Papers, 1st U.S.C.I., RG 94: Records of the Adjutants General's Office, 1780-1917, NA.

8. Berlin, *Destruction of Slavery*, 166, 335-37; Berlin, *Free At Last*, 59-60; McPherson, *Battle Cry of Freedom*, 499-502, 557-58. The Second Confiscation Act, the Militia Act, and the Preliminary Emancipation Proclamation offered fugitive slaves their freedom and thus greatly encouraged slaves to escape.

9. Berlin, *Destruction of Slavery*, 5. McPherson, *Battle Cry of Freedom*, 464-78, 538-45 discusses the Seven Days' Battles and the Battle of Antietam. Deposition of Francis Marshall, January 9, 1884, Pension File of Francis Marshall, RG 15, NA.

10. Berlin, et al., eds., *Destruction of Slavery*, 3; Deposition of Nancy Dixon, April 4, 1881, Pension File of Richard Dixon, RG 15, NA; Deposition of Harriet Williams, July 31, 1886, Pension File Richard Dixon, RG 15, NA. Harriet Williams, Dixon's sister, stated that the slaves cared for the ill Stringfellow and the farm until Stringfellow fled. Stringfellow allowed the slaves to raise crops and livestock for personal use and consumption. Nancy Dixon, Richard's mother, was the pension claimant in this case.

11. Deposition of George H. Boston, October 25, 1900, Pension File of George H. Boston, RG 15, NA. Dominick Bolin owned the plantation on which Boston was raised and the plantation from which Boston escaped. For information regarding the hazards

fugitives faced in Maryland, see Berlin, et al., eds., *Destruction of Slavery*, 334-36; and Fields, *Slavery and Freedom on the Middle Ground*, 118-19.

12. Deposition of George Washington Berry, May 11, 1900, Pension File of George Brent, RG 15, NA. Deposition of George Brent, September 11, 1899, Pension File of George Brent, RG 15, NA.

13. Deposition of Welcome Lee, December 4, 1888, Pension File of Welcome Lee, RG 15, NA.

14. Deposition of Armstead Bond, October 29, 1900, Pension File of Armstead Bond, RG 15, NA; Berlin, et al., eds., *Destruction of Slavery*, 59-61.

15. Ira Berlin, Joseph P. Reidy, and Leslie S. Rowland, eds., *Freedom: A Documentary History of Emancipation*, 1861-1867, ser. II. vol. I, *The Black Military Experience* (Cambridge: 1982), 129.

16. Handon Hargrove, *Black Union Soldiers in the Civil War* (Jefferson, North Carolina: 1988), 71-84; Green, *The Secret City*, 70; Leech, *Reveille in Washington*, 236-41; "The Colored Regiment," *The Evening Star*, May 5, 1863; "Washington Correspondence," *Christian Recorder*, June 13, 1863, "The Colored Volunteer," *National Republican*, May 12, 1863; "The Colored Regiment," *National Republican*, May 23; "Another War Meeting of Colored Men," *National Republican*, May 19, 1863. Several meetings took place at the Israel Bethel Church, Big Bethel Church, John Wesley Church, and First Baptist Church of Washington.

17. Dudley T. Cornish, *The Sable Arm: Black Troops in the Union Army, 1861-1865* (Lawrence:1956), 130; and Joseph T. Glatthaar, *Forged in Battle: The Civil War Alliance of Black Soldiers and White Officers* (New York: 1990), 10, 38-39, provides insightful treatments of the Bureau of Colored Troops and its functions. "Invading Sacred Soil," *Evening Star*, May 22, 1863, describes the regiment's move to Mason's Island. Deposition of George Boston, September 3, 1890, Pension Files of George Boston, RG 15, NA. Maj. C. H. Raymond Asst. Adj. Gen. to Col. John Holman, July 7, 1863, Regimental Order Book, Regimental Books and Papers, 1st U.S.C.I., RG 94, NA. John Holman, originally from Boston, Mass., received a second lieutenant's commission in the Missouri Reserve Militia in 1861 and later a lieutenant colonelcy in the 26th Missouri Infantry. John Holman Papers, Western Historical Manuscript Collection, University of Missouri.

18. Deposition of George H. Boston, October 25, 1900, Pension File of George H. Boston, RG 15, NA; Deposition of George Hatton, December 26, 1900, Pension File of George Hatton, RG 15, NA; Deposition of Charles Gurtrige, March 8, 1898, Pension Files of Charles Gurtrige, RG 15, NA; Deposition of Armstead Bond, October 29, 1900, Pension File of Armstead Bond, RG 15, NA.

19. *Evening Times*, May 22, 1863, "A Soldier Too"; *National Republican*, June 12, 1863, "Policeman Arrested"; McPherson, *The Negro's Civil War*, 163-64 and 178-81; *Christian Recorder*, July 4, 1863, "From Washington." For more information involving hostile actions against the recruits of the 1st U.S.C.T. see Leech, *Reveille in Washington*, 152-54.

20. First Sgt. Lincoln Lewis, Regimental Logs, Regimental Books and Papers, 1st U.S.C.I., RG 94, NA. Lewis noted that the regiment left for Fort Monroe at 8:00 a.m. on August 3, 1863.

21. Ira Berlin, et. al., *The Black Military Experience*, 363-64.

22. First Sgt. Lincoln Lewis, Regimental Log Book, Regimental Books and Papers, 1st U.S.C.I., RG 94 NA. Lewis logged the daily movements of the regiment from August 4, 1863, to August 11, 1863; Lewis was a free-born mulatto shoemaker from Charleston, S.C., who joined the regiment in May 1863. The affidavit of Welcome Lee, June 19, 1888, Pension File of Welcome Lee, RG 15, NA. Lee was a fugitive slave from Elizabeth City, North Carolina. In 1862, he escaped to Roanoke Island and then to Washington, D.C., where he worked for the Quartermasters Corps before enlisting. In the *Christian Recorder*, September 19, 1963, "Plymouth, North Carolina," Sgt. John Tunnia, a native of Washington, D.C., gives a sketchy account of the trip from Mason's Island to Plymouth and expresses his and the regiment's anger over the pay situation.

23. Col. Holman to Maj. C. W. Foster, Asst. Adj. Gen., December 23, 1863, 1st U.S.C.I. Letters Sent, Regimental Books and Papers, RG 94, NA; Col. John Holman to Lt. H. W. Allen, Asst. Adj. Gen, Dept Of Virginia. and North Carolina, November 15, 1863, 1st U.S.C.I., Letters Sent, Regimental Books and Papers, RG 94, NA; Special Order no.[74], November 10, 1863, 1st U.S.C.I., Regimental Order Book, Regimental Books and Papers, RG 94, NA.

24. John G. Barrett, *The Civil War in North Carolina* (Chapel Hill: 1963), 177-81.

25. Ibid., 179; Deposition of Theodore Ray, May 12, 1887, Pension Files of Theodore Ray, RG15, NA; Deposition of John Brown, April 4, Pension Files of John Brown, RG 15, NA; Col. Holman to Maj. Davis, Asst. Adj. Gen. of Dept. of Virginia and North Carolina, Letters Sent, Regimental Books and Papers, 1st U.S.C.I., RG 94, NA; Col. Holman, Regimental Order No. 68, Regimental Order Book, Regimental Books and Papers, 1st U.S.C.I., RG 94, NA; General Affidavit of John Haynes, September 17, 1888, Pension Files of John Haynes, RG 15, NA.

26. Regimental Order Book, Regimental Books and Papers, 1st U.S.C.I., RG 94, NA.

27. Regimental Order Book, Regimental Books and Papers, 1st U.S.C.I., RG 94, NA; Barrett, *Civil War in North Carolina*, 179.

28. Order no. 69, January 3, 1863, Regimental Order Book, Regimental Books and Papers, 1st U.S.C.I., RG 94, NA. In this order, Holman commended the troops for their "soldierly bearing" and "overcoming the obstacles" faced by black troops. The morning reports provide a daily list of men assigned to the various details. See Morning Reports and Order Book, Regimental Books and Papers, 1st U.S.C.I., RG 94, NA.

29. First Sgt. Lincoln Lewis, Regimental Log Book, Regimental Books and Papers, 1st U.S.C.I., RG 94, NA; *Christian Recorder*, April 16, 1864, "Letter From New Bern, North Carolina."

30. Brig. Gen. E. A. Wild, Special Order No. 32, February 12, 1864, 1st U.S.C.I., Regimental Order Book, Regimental Books and Papers, RG 94, NA; 1st. Sgt. Lincoln

Lewis, Regimental Log, Regimental Books and Papers, RG 94, NA; *Christian Recorder*, April 16, 1864, "Letter From New Bern, North Carolina"; and May 7, 1864, "For the Christian Recorder." U.S. War Department, *The War of the Rebellion: The Official Records of the Union and Confederate Armies*, 128 vols. (Washington, D.C., 1890 -1901), Series I, vol. 33, 303-4 and 966. Herinafter cited as *OR*. All references are to series I unless otherwise noted.

31. Pvt. James McDonald, a free-born shoemaker from Loudon Co., Va, testified that the regiment received new muskets at Fortress Monroe in the spring of 1864. Deposition of James McDonald, March 3, 1911, Pension Files of James McDonald, RG 15, NA. See *Christian Recorder*, May 7, 1864, "For the Christian Recorder." Hatton describes his thoughts when the regiment joins the Army of the James at City Point. He also states that the regiment was preparing for a "great raid" near Richmond. See also *OR* 36, pt. 2, 165.

32. *Christian Recorder*, May 28, 1864, "Retaliation In Camp."

33. Turner's account of the Battle of Wilson's Wharf was carried in the *Christian Recorder*, June 25, 1864, "From Chaplin Turner." Also see *OR* 36, part II, 270-71.

34. Handon B. Hargrove, *Black Union Soldiers in the Civil War, 1862-63*; James M. McPherson, *Battle Cry of Freedom: The Civil War Era* (Oxford: 1988), 740-41; *OR* 51, pt. 1, 263-67.; *OR* 40, pt. 1, 720-23.

35. Hargrove, *Black Union Soldiers in the Civil War*, 182-83; McPherson, *Battle Cry of Freedom*, 740-41; *OR* 51, pt. 1, 263-67; *OR* 40, pt. 1, 720-23; *Christian Recorder*, July, 9, 1864, "A Very Important Letter From Chaplin Turner"; Deposition of George Boston, October 25, 1900, Pension Files of George Boston, RG 15, NA.

36. *Christian Recorder*, July, 9, 1864, "A Very Important Letter From Chaplin Turner."

37. *Christian Recorder*, July 9, 1864, "For The Christian Recorder;" *Christian Recorder*, August 20, 1864, "From City Point."

38. McPherson, *Battle Cry of Freedom*, 740-78; Dyer, *A Compendium*, 1,723; Glatthaar, *Forged in Battle*, 150-51; Cornish, *Sable Arm* , 278-83; *OR* 42, pt. 2, 101; *OR* 42, pt. 1, 136; Deposition of James Roberts, August 1, 1900, Pension Files of James Roberts, RG 15, NA; Deposition of Buck Hedgeman, December 18, 1892, Pension Files of Buck Hedgeman, RG 15, NA. Hedgeman was a sharpshooter from the 1st U.S.C.I.; Deposition of James Adams, August 1, 1900, Pension File of James Adams, RG 15, NA.

39. Cornish, *Sable Arm*, 280-281; *OR* 42, pt. 1, 151, 814-17. Deposition of John Minus, December 27, 1901, Pension File of John W. Minus, RG 15, NA. R. J. M. Blackett, Thomas Morris Chester: *Black Civil War Correspondent, His Dispatches from the Virginia Front* (Baton Rouge: 1989), 171-84.

40. *Christian Recorder*, July 16, 1864, "Everybody Read This"; and September 24, 1864, "Army Correspondent."; *OR* 42, pt. 2, 208.; Deposition of Richard Parker, August 23, 1892, Pension File of Richard Parker, RG 15, NA; Affidavit of Nicholas Larney, August 19, 1864, Pension File of Joseph Taylor, RG 15, NA.

41. *Christian Recorder*, July 16, 1864, "Everybody Read This"; September 24, 1864, "Army Correspondence"; and October 8, 1864, "Army Correspondence."

42. McPherson, *Battle Cry of Freedom*, 819-21.; *Christian Recorder*, January 7 and 14, 1865, "Notes By The Way To Wilmington"; Deposition of James Adams, August 31, 1900, Pension Files of James Adams; Deposition of David Livers, February 27, 1891, Pension File of David Livers, RG 15, NA.

43. *OR* 46, pt. 1, 143; *OR* 47, pt. 1, 924-26. The XXV Army Corps consisted of nine black infantry regiments, three white artillery batteries, and two white companies of engineers. Deposition of John Morgan, June 2, 1904, Pension File of John Minus. RG 15, NA. Morgan "strained" his right side building breastworks near Wilmington the day before the fort's capture.

44. McPherson, *Battle Cry of Freedom*, 820-22; Barrett, *Civil War in North Carolina*, 272-78.

45. *OR* 47, pt. 1, 924-26.

46. Ibid.

47. Ibid. 926-27; Deposition of John Tunnia, November 21, 1892, Pension Files of John Tunnia, RG 15, NA

48. *Christian Recorder*, April 15, 1865, "Army Correspondence By Chaplain Turner."

49. Ibid.

50. Berlin, *The Black Military Experience*, 733-37; *Christian Recorder*, June, 10, 1865, "Army Correspondence." See Glatthaar, *Forged in Battle*, 210-21, for a detailed discussion of black troops during Reconstruction.

51. *Christian Recorder*, May 6, 1865, "Army Correspondence"

52. *Christian Recorder*, May 27, 1865, "Army Correspondence"; and June 10, 1865, "Army Correspondence."

53. *Christian Recorder*, June 24, 1865, "Army Correspondence By Chaplain Turner"; and July 1, 1865, "Army Correspondence."

54. Col. Holman to Capt. Carter, Asst. Adj. Gen., June 23, 1865, Letters Sent, Regimental Books and Papers, 1st U.S.C.I., RG 94, NA; Lt. Nathan Bishop, Adj. 1st U.S.C.I. to Magistrates and Leading Men of Hyde County, Aug. 23, 1865, Letters Sent, Regimental Books and Papers, 1st U.S.C.I., RG 94, NA; Col. Holman to Capt. W. L. Goodrich, Sept. 12, 1865, Letters Sent, Regimental Books and Papers, 1st. U.S.C.I., RG 94, NA.

55. *Christian Recorder*, May 27, 1865, "Army Correspondence."

56. Dyer, *A Compendium*, 1,723. *Evening Star*, October 9, 1865, "Arrival of the First District Colored Regiment."

"MAKING THE OBSTINATE STAND"

The Battle of Town Creek and the Fall of Wilmington

Chris E. Fonvielle, Jr.

B rigadier General Johnson Hagood's appointed task of halting the Union juggernaut on the west side of the murky Cape Fear River was unenviable. Duty compelled Hagood and his motley brigade of South Carolina infantrymen and North Carolina artillerymen to try and stop a far superior number of blue-clad soldiers determined to capture Wilmington, North Carolina. But the situation appeared daunting for the South Carolina planter-turned-soldier.

The Confederates already had lost Fort Fisher—the strongest seacoast fortification in the Confederacy and the main guardian of Wilmington— to the largest Union army-navy operation of the war. The loss of Fisher in mid-January 1865 closed the last gateway to Confederate blockade running on the Atlantic seaboard and portended the South's collapse. Indeed, Robert E. Lee himself had cautioned military authorities that should his lifeline through Wilmington be severed, he could not maintain his army in Virginia.

The Union high command, however, was not content with just sealing the Confederacy's last major seaport to overseas trade. Now they cast their covetous gaze on Wilmington, tapped by three major railroads and the Cape Fear River which was navigable for 100 miles into the state's interior. Possession of these vital lines of communication would enable the federals to reinforce and resupply Gen. William T. Sherman's army, then advancing through the Carolinas *en route* to Virginia. Sherman planned to link his force with U. S. Grant's two operational

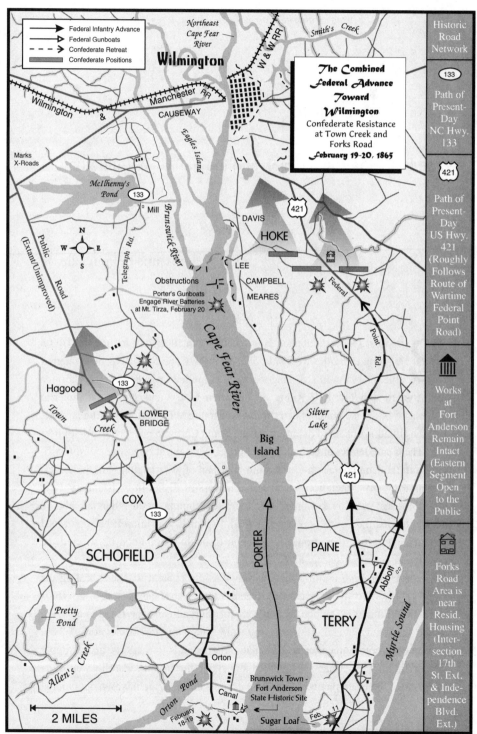

Federal Infantry Advance
Federal Gunboats
Confederate Retreat
Confederate Positions

The Combined
Federal Advance
Toward
Wilmington
Confederate Resistance
at Town Creek and
Forks Road
February 19-20, 1865

Northeast
Cape Fear
River

Smith's Creek

Wilmington

W & W RR

Wilmington & Manchester RR

CAUSEWAY

Eagles Island

Marks
X-Roads

McIlhenny's
Pond   133

Mill

Brunswick River

N
W   E
S

DAVIS

HOKE

LEE

CAMPBELL

MEARES

Federal

Obstructions
Porter's Gunboats
Engage River Batteries
at Mt. Tirza, February 20

Cape Fear River

Point Rd.

Telegraph Rd.

Public Road
(Extant/Unimproved)

Hagood

133

LOWER
BRIDGE

Town
Creek

Silver
Lake

Big
Island

421

COX

133

SCHOFIELD

PORTER

PAINE

Abbott

Pretty
Pond

Allen's Creek

Orton

Orton
Pond
Canal

Brunswick Town -
Fort Anderson
State Historic Site

February
18-19

Sugar Loaf

Feb. 11

TERRY

Myrtle Sound

2 MILES

Adapted from *Moore's Historical Guide to the Wilmington Campaign & the Battles for Fort Fisher* (Forthcoming from Savas Publishing)   Mark A. Moore

*Historic
Road
Network*

133

*Path of
Present-
Day
NC Hwy.
133*

421

*Path of
Present-
Day
US Hwy.
421
(Roughly
Follows
Route of
Wartime
Federal
Point
Road)*

*Works
at
Fort
Anderson
Remain
Intact
(Eastern
Segment
Open
to the
Public*

*Forks
Road
Area is
near
Resid.
Housing
(Inter-
section
17th
St. Ext.
& Inde-
pendence
Blvd.
Ext.)*

commands—the Army of the Potomac and the Army of the James—for a final showdown with Lee's Army of Northern Virginia, bottle necked between Petersburg and Richmond. General Grant therefore deemed "the capture of Wilmington of the greatest importance" to Sherman's campaign and to ending the four-year-long conflict.

After reinforcements arrived in the Lower Cape Fear in early February 1865, 15,000 Union troops moved rapidly in two wings toward the Carolina port town. A flotilla of about thirty Union gunboats ascended the river in support of the U.S. Army's advance up both sides of the waterway. The massive expeditionary force included 6,500 infantrymen of Maj. Gen. Jacob D. Cox's four brigades of the Second and Third Divisions, XXIII Army Corps deployed on the west bank of the Cape Fear River.

Major General Robert F. Hoke, temporary commander of the Cape Fear District, assigned General Johnson Hagood with a vastly outnumbered force of about 2,300 North Carolina and South Carolina soldiers to stop Cox's movement. But supported by naval gunfire, Cox outflanked Hagood at Fort Anderson, a huge earthen fort that covered the western approaches to Wilmington. Hagood was forced to flee northward, taking up a line of defense at Town Creek halfway between Fort Anderson and the city. Town Creek represented the final bit of defensible terrain west of the Cape Fear River. Here the South Carolinian planned to make a more determined stand.[1]

Hagood's command crossed lower Town Creek bridge just before 10:00 a.m. on February 19, and assumed a position on the north bank. Hagood placed Col. John J. Hedrick in command at the bridge, which was defended by Lt. Col. John Douglas Taylor's battalion of North Carolinians and three pieces of artillery (including a Whitworth rifle cannon) in entrenchments on a bluff overlooking the span. Hagood held the bulk of his force near a small clapboard church half a mile north of the bridge. A mounted party of twenty gray-clad men, commanded by a Lieutenant Jeffords, patrolled the road south of the creek to watch for the approaching Federals.[2]

Soon after Hagood's force reached lower Town Creek, Col. Thomas J. Lipscomb reported that he and his 2nd South Carolina Cavalry, together with a howitzer and small crew of artillerymen, had reached upper Town Creek bridge seven miles to the northwest. Hagood directed Lipscomb to scout his front and along the creek between the two bridges. As soon as his troops were deployed, Hagood telegraphed Hoke for instructions. "Future operations will depend on circumstances," Hoke replied from his headquarters near Wilmington. "Will tele-

Brig. Genl. Johnson Hagood, the defender of Fort Anderson and the Town Creek line, in a beautiful and previously unpublished image. *U.S. Army Military History Institute*

graph you in the morning." For the moment Hagood could only await the Federal advance.[3]

The Palmetto State general faced no immediate threat. The burned bridge and cut sluices at the Orton Pond canal near Fort Anderson had retarded the Union pursuit, and his position at Town Creek was a strong one. Named for an ill-fated English settlement in the 1660s, Town Creek was narrow but deep and unfordable, with wide marshes and vast rice fields and dikes on both sides. An occasional wooded bluff touched the stream here and there, but the two bridges were the only regular crossings. Both spans had been lightly fortified earlier and were now adequately defended. Hagood also controlled two possible avenues of retreat, the Public Road (the main thoroughfare to Wilmington), and the Telegraph Road, an aptly named byway closer to the Cape Fear River along which a telegraph line ran to the city, eight miles upriver.[4]

Believing Wilmington was within their grasp, Gen. Jacob D. Cox's brigades reached lower Town Creek bridge at about 3:30 in the afternoon on February 19. The approaching vanguard—Col. Thomas J. Henderson's Third Brigade, Third Division—had been ordered to "move cautiously and to advance as near to the enemy as practicable before night." Henderson's men met little opposition until they neared the bridge, where Henderson found a "strong rebel picket." This force was Lieutenant Jeffords' mounted troopers, who on Hagood's orders retired to the safety of the north side of the stream after a round of light skirmishing. The Confederates pulled up the planks of the bridge as they retreated, but did not have enough time to destroy the span.[5]

Colonel Henderson deployed his infantry on a sand ridge half a mile south of the creek and set about fortifying his position. A few Confederate artillery shells came crashing down, though most passed harmlessly overhead and exploded in the rear. As ordered, Henderson had driven his brigade "as near to the enemy as practicable," and could go no further. While Confederate sharpshooters tried to pick off Henderson's skirmishers advancing into the bulrush bordering the stream, the colonel surveyed the scene before him. He described this portion of Hagood's new defensive line as a "very strong position, complete with heavy works and. . .three pieces of artillery." The creek before him was "not wide, but deep," he related, "and could not be passed by troops without a bridge or a boat." Further complicating matters was a large and impassable marsh, which covered the line between Henderson and the creek. There was only one viable route over Town Creek, and that was over the causeway and into the teeth of the Southern defenses. While Henderson pondered his options, the brigades of Cols. Orlando

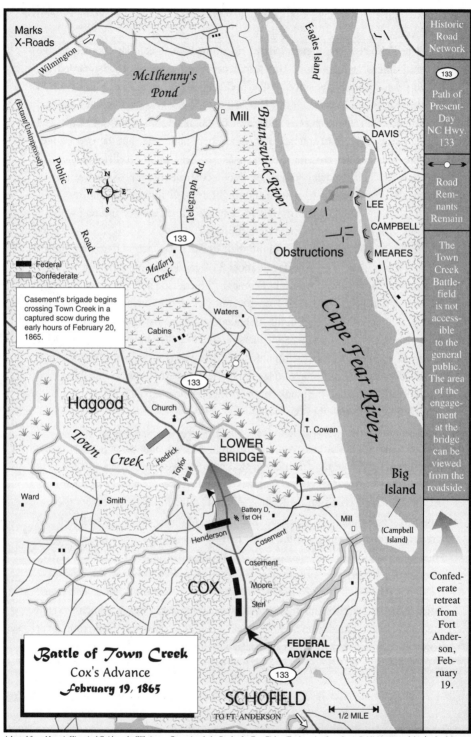

Marks
X-Roads

Wilmington

(Extant/Unimproved)

McIlhenny's
Pond

Mill

Brunswick River

Eagles Island

DAVIS

Public
Road

Telegraph Rd.

133

LEE

CAMPBELL

MEARES

Obstructions

Federal
Confederate

Mallory
Creek

Casement's brigade begins
crossing Town Creek in a
captured scow during the
early hours of February 20,
1865.

Waters

Cabins

Cape Fear River

133

Hagood

Church

T. Cowan

Town Creek

Hedrick

LOWER
BRIDGE

Big
Island

Taylor

Ward   Smith

Battery D,
1st OH

Mill

(Campbell
Island)

Henderson

Casement

Casement

COX

Moore

Sterl

Battle of Town Creek
Cox's Advance
February 19, 1865

FEDERAL
ADVANCE

133

SCHOFIELD

TO FT. ANDERSON   1/2 MILE

Historic
Road
Network

133

Path of
Present-
Day
NC Hwy.
133

Road
Rem-
nants
Remain

The
Town
Creek
Battle-
field
is not
access-
ible
to the
general
public.
The area
of the
engage-
ment
at the
bridge
can be
viewed
from the
roadside.

Confed-
erate
retreat
from
Fort
Ander-
son,
Feb-
ruary
19.

Adapted from *Moore's Historical Guide to the Wilmington Campaign & the Battles for Fort Fisher* (Forthcoming from Savas Publishing)   Mark A. Moore

Moore, Oscar W. Sterl, and John S. Casement, remained out of sight and under cover in Henderson's rear.[6]

With light skirmishing in his front, Hagood telegraphed the developing situation to Robert Hoke at 5:35 p.m. "Town Creek is a line [that] can be held whenever occupied," he cautiously stated, making it clear immediately thereafter that he did not have enough men to hold the entire line. "I have examined several miles of it today," he continued. "From my observation it can be crossed almost anywhere that sufficient troops are not stationed. Let me know your views and intentions." Hoke's response later that night was simply: "Hold Town Creek till you hear from me." Hagood's new position at Town Creek was uncomfortably similar to the dreadful situation he had just left behind at Fort Anderson, seven miles to the south. He had a wide front with too few troops to hold it, and an aggressive enemy itching to force a crossing and cut his path to Wilmington. Those same circumstances had compelled Hagood to abandon Fort Anderson, a large earthen fortification guarding Wilmington's western approaches, earlier that morning, February 19.[7]

Instructed by his superior officer to hold the Town Creek line, General Hagood deployed the 11th South Carolina Infantry about dark on February 19 to picket the two-and-a-half mile stretch of ground along the stream from the lower bridge to the Cape Fear River. The soldiers were to guard against a flanking movement by the Union army or a landing of sailors and marines. Yet Hagood's fears about a naval landing party were unfounded. The U. S. Navy still was smarting from the debacle its shore contingent had suffered at Fort Fisher. Even if a force should come ashore, it was a long way from the river to Hagood's position across ground unfamiliar to the Union sailors and marines.[8]

While Johnson Hagood contemplated his own state of affairs, Jacob Cox sent reconnaissance parties to search for a place to ford Town Creek. As Colonel Henderson was just discovering and Cox's scouts would soon learn, the stream was not fordable. Cox faced a dilemma. Confederate guns swept the lower bridge's only approach—a long corduroy causeway through a wide marsh of tall reeds. The only other span, which Cox assumed the Confederates had already destroyed, was seven miles upstream to the northwest. Moreover, getting pontoons ashore appeared impractical. The Cape Fear River was wide where Town Creek emptied into it, and the pontoon-laden ships were in the channel on the east side of Campbell Island. While Cox pondered a course of action, fate intervened on his behalf.

After dark, an elderly black man approached Colonel Henderson to inform him of a rice barge that was docked at a warehouse on the south side of Town

Creek about one and a half-miles downstream. The Confederates had overlooked it when they had crossed the creek earlier that morning. Henderson sent
word of his discovery to General Cox, who immediately ordered that the flatboat be confiscated. Cox in turn notified Maj. Gen. John M. Schofield, commander of the Department of North Carolina and headquartered on the S. R.
Spaulding on the Cape Fear River, recommending that the scow be used to
outflank the Confederates. Schofield approved Cox's suggestion by telling him
to "see what could be done with the flat boat."[9]

Before sunrise the next morning, Cox sent Casement's and Sterl's brigades
to make the crossing. It was slow going. The flatboat could carry only fifty or so
men at a time, and when the soldiers disembarked on the north side of the
stream, they had to wade a considerable distance through rice paddies, marsh,
and muck before reaching dry ground. By 11:00 a.m., only Casement's brigade
had been ferried across. The unsupported soldiers erected crude breastworks as
they anxiously waited for their comrades to follow them.[10]

At daylight Colonel Henderson sent out a strong skirmish line toward the
bridge to divert Hagood's attention from the Federal flanking movement. Henderson's skirmishers advanced into the low ground along the creek, though the
marsh grass offered the Federals little protection against the Confederates'
heavy small arms and artillery fire. Even so, one Union officer claimed that the
sharpshooters "succeeded in getting so close to the creek as to prevent any of the
enemy from showing themselves above the parapet." To cover his skirmishers,
Colonel Henderson ordered Lt. Cecil C. Reed's Battery D, 1st Ohio Artillery, to
fire upon the enemy. Reed deployed his battery of 3-inch Parrott rifles in the
road bed, giving him a clearer shot at the Confederate defenses on the north
bank. "Our artillery opened upon them, causing them to scatter," observed a
Confederate officer. "In a few moments they returned the fire with rifle guns &
it was now our time to scatter." For the remainder of the day the fighting across
the stream became "brisk and animated, enlivened by occasional duels between
the Union and Confederate artillery."[11]

From his headquarters at Forks Road three miles south of Wilmington,
General Hoke could hear the din of battle raging on the opposite side of the
river. At some point during the day Hoke telegraphed General Hagood, "You
must move your command as you think best; at same time recollect the importance of your communication with Wilmington. . .I leave the matter to your
judgment." Hoke followed this rather vague directive with more definitive instructions later that day when he ordered Hagood to "dispute their advance at
every available point." Wilmington had to be held longer than anticipated. The

Maj. Gen. Jacob D. Cox, the able and respected commander of four brigades of the U.S.
XXIII Army Corps at Town Creek. *U.S. Army Military History Institute*

removal of government property and thousands of Union prisoners-of-war sent to Wilmington for exchange had bogged down efforts to evacuate the city. Moreover, Lt. Gen. William J. Hardee had requested Hoke's assistance in transporting his army to Greensboro by way of Wilmington. Sherman's surge through South Carolina had forced Hardee's evacuation of Charleston three days earlier. "Old Reliable" Hardee was now retreating northward along the Northeastern Railroad and gradually approaching Wilmington. Hoke believed he could effect Hardee's passage through the port town so long as Hagood held Town Creek and protected the Wilmington & Manchester rail line, which ran roughly parallel to Hagood's position several miles to his rear. Although Hoke had hoped to battle it out with Schofield, he now focused his efforts on holding on just long enough to enable Hardee's Corps to withdraw to Greensboro via Wilmington.[12]

The crafty Jacob D. Cox broke the frustrating stalemate by again outwitting Johnson Hagood and flanking his force. By early afternoon on February 20, the brigades of Colonels Sterl and Moore had joined Colonel Casement's regiments on the north bank of Town Creek. General Cox had decided at the last moment to strike Hagood with three of his brigades rather than two, and he personally took command of the movement. Having missed the chance to spring a similar trap he had set at Fort Anderson the previous day, "this time Genl Cox was determined to catch something," a young Northern soldier wrote home to his parents.[13]

Fortunately for Cox, Hagood's pickets had not detected the crossing. Apparently the Confederates assumed the deep creek and swampy terrain would prevent the enemy from gaining their flank, and as a result, there were not enough pickets posted along the stream. During the morning of February 20, Capt. Joseph J. Wescoat and Abram W. Clement of the 11th South Carolina Infantry walked down from their picket camp to Town Creek in order to forage for food. The two soldiers had heard rumors that a load of sweet potatoes and barrels of apple cider were at a landing near the videttes' forward position. The sight of Union warships in the river discouraged Wescoat and Clement from raiding nearby Cowan's plantation (which was rich with livestock) because they feared their appearance in the yard might draw the fire of the gunboats. Instead they moved on to the landing, where they found the flatboat, and soon filled their haversacks with potatoes and their canteens with cider. They had just returned to their encampment and were feasting on their plunder when a report came in that the pickets they had left a short time before had been surprised and captured by Union forces. Captain Wescoat retraced his route to the creek, only to discover Union troops assembling *en masse*. Wescoat turned and dashed off on horseback to alert General Hagood.[14]

About 10:00 a.m. that morning, Col. Charles H. Simonton, the field commander of Hagood's Brigade, had dispatched the 21st and 25th South Carolina Infantry from their position near the lower bridge to relieve the 11th South Carolina on picket duty near Cowan's plantation. Soon thereafter, Simonton witnessed Captain Wescoat's frantic ride into camp and hasty conversation with General Hagood, only to watch him gallop off again a short time later. Sensing something was amiss, Simonton responded immediately to the general's call for him to come to headquarters at the church. Simonton learned of Wescoat's report and was instructed by Hagood to go at once to Cowan's, taking with him the 27th South Carolina Infantry and two pieces of North Carolina artillery under Lt. John T. Rankin. He was also to retain the two South Carolina units he had sent in that direction earlier, as well as the 11th South Carolina Infantry already on patrol. Hagood suggested "that it would be best to attack."[15]

Two lanes led from the Telegraph Road to the mouth of Town Creek. The southernmost lane, Cowan's Road, intersected the telegraph road about a mile north of lower Town Creek bridge. Another road joined the Telegraph Road about half a mile further to the north, running roughly parallel to the river and past Cowan's plantation before intersecting with Cowan's Road near the mouth of the creek.[16] Using Cowan's Road, Simonton soon reached the reserve picket station about two miles from Hagood's headquarters, where he discovered that the Federals had already driven Captain Wescoat's skirmishers 300 yards west of Cowan's gate, and were forming for battle. Simonton hurriedly deployed his troops to check the enemy's advance, placing the 27th South Carolina in line of battle on the right side of Cowan's Road, the 11th South Carolina to the left, and Lieutenant Rankin's artillery on the lane. The 21st and 25th South Carolina regiments were sent forward as skirmishers.

Desiring a good look at the enemy, Simonton soon joined the skirmishers and managed to move so close to the enemy that he could distinctly hear officers barking orders to their men. He was astounded by the large number of Union troops, and quickly sent word to Hagood that a "considerable" enemy force was at that moment in his front along the south lane and preparing to advance. Simonton prudently withdrew his force about thirty yards, placing what he described as a "sort of pond" between him and the enemy. When the Federals failed to immediately launch their attack, Simonton returned to the skirmish line, accompanied by Capt. William E. Stoney, a member of General Hagood's staff who had come down from headquarters to assess the situation. By then, however,

Previously unpublished image of Lt. John T. Rankin, who was captured with his command of North Carolina artillerymen in hand-to-hand fighting against Gen. Jacob D. Cox's Union troops at Town Creek on February 20, 1865.

Courtesy of the author

most of the Union troops were moving to envelop Simonton's flanks, particularly his left flank in an effort to gain the north road. When the movement was discovered, Simonton had no choice but to retreat.[17]

Sensing urgency in Simonton's report when it arrived at headquarters, General Hagood decided to go in person to Cowan's to investigate. Simonton was still on the skirmish line when Hagood arrived at the front. Simonton's troops were caught in a sharp skirmish with Cox's force, which Hagood realized was endeavoring to overlap the South Carolinians flanks. Only the threat of Rankin's artillery, deployed on Cowan's Road, held Cox at bay.

A quick reconnaissance convinced Hagood that Cox had managed to out-flank him again, just as he had at Fort Anderson. The Federals were now in control of the mouth of Town Creek and, with naval support, could fling their entire force across the stream at any time. Hagood, of course, did not know that the bulk of Cox's division was already on the north side of the creek. He did realize, however, that the enemy force constituted a serious threat to his ability to hold his present position. The Town Creek line must be abandoned at once, Hagood concluded, but he needed time to alert his scattered troops and effect a withdrawal.

Hagood redeployed the 27th South Carolina to the left of Cowan's Road and personally led the 11th South Carolina back to the Telegraph Road, positioning it slightly south of the intersection with Cowan's. After establishing this new line, Hagood returned to Simonton's position, where that officer was trying to keep his small force of some 450 soldiers from disintegrating under the mounting pressure of the oncoming Union tide. Hagood ordered Simonton to delay Cox's advance for as long as possible in order to give the main Confederate force at the bridge time to retreat up the Public Road to Wilmington. The South Carolina brigadier instructed Simonton to deploy his force so as to guard both roads and to fall back slowly, contesting every foot of ground. Simonton was to concentrate his troops and artillery when he reached the Telegraph Road. Hagood would be close by to help support his return to the main army.

Hagood hastened back to his headquarters at the church, taking one piece of Rankin's artillery with him as far as the Telegraph Road to cover Simonton's retreat at that point. Colonel Lipscomb, who had seen no action at all at the upper bridge, was ordered to retire with his force at once to Marks Cross Roads just outside of Wilmington. The general also sent his wagon train, artillery and sick and wounded to Wilmington. Two men were ordered to burn the bridge at McIl-henny's millpond and to cut the sluices to prevent the Federals from using the Telegraph Road to intercept the Confederate retreat to Wilmington via the Public

Road. At 3:00 p.m. Hagood directed Colonel Hedrick to start withdrawing his force from the lower bridge. From the sound of heavy rifle musket fire to the east, Hagood knew that Simonton was being hard pressed. "I am now evacuating," Hagood wired General Hoke. "Enemy are turning my flank and are pushing me too strong." Hagood ended his telegram with "Am obliged to do so," as if he felt a need to emphasize that he was giving up the position against his will.[18]

Simonton's small force put up a good fight, but Cox's division heavily outnumbered the Confederates' over-stretched and worn out force. The Federal general pushed Simonton all afternoon, concentrating his troops on the north road to gain Hagood's rear. Infantry from the 65th Indiana deployed as skirmishers, supported by nine other regiments of Casement's and Sterl's brigades, which were drawn up in a double line of battle on the left side of the road. Colonel Moore's brigade brought up the rear of Cox's force, marching in column on the road. The Federals steadily pushed back Simonton's South Carolinians, although their advance was impeded by swamps and thick woods with ensnarled tangled undergrowth.[19]

As Hagood had instructed, Simonton stretched his thin line of troops to cover both lanes and slowly fell back. By about 4:30 p.m. the enemy had skirmished their way to the Telegraph Road, where Simonton planned to make a more determined stand. Here the terrain changed from thick woods and low ground to a flat sand plain covered with sedge broom grass and scattered turkey oaks and pine trees—an ideal setting for a battle. Simonton pulled his scattered troops together and advanced the 11th South Carolina from the point where Hagood had placed it south of Cowan's Road. A new line of battle was formed straddling the Telegraph Road and facing north toward Cox's brigades, which were now concentrating their weight on the north road. Simonton pushed the 21st South Carolina into the wooded fields deployed as a strong force of skirmishers. The Carolinians were instructed to form at right angles on the flanks of his line of battle if the Federals overlapped his front.[20]

Colonel Simonton was supported by Lieutenant Rankin's two field pieces, including a bronze 12-pounder howitzer that its crew—members of Company B, 3rd Battalion North Carolina Light Artillery—had nicknamed "St. Paul." The gun and three others like it had been cast at Richmond's Tredegar Iron Works early in the war from bells that had hung in churches, schools, the courthouse, and the shipyard in Edenton, North Carolina, which explained the unit's unusual nickname: the Edenton Bell Battery. With "St. Paul" and one other field piece now on the line at Town Creek, Simonton and his men hastily erected crude

Lt. William Calder
1st Battalion, North Carolina Heavy Artillery

Robert Calder

breastworks and awaited the enemy's attack or Hagood's order to retreat—whichever came first.[21]

After reaching the Telegraph Road, General Cox learned from some blacks
who lived nearby that Hagood's main body of troops was on the Public Road,
further to the west. Armed with this valuable information, Cox ordered Colonel
Moore to rush his brigade through the swamp between the two roads and cut off
Hagood's retreat. As Moore moved out, both Casement's and Sterl's brigades
were sent forward against Simonton's contingent standing between Cox and
Town Creek.[22]

As Simonton gallantly stood his ground, General Hagood ordered the remainder of his troops at the lower bridge to retire. A "hurried flight from the
trenches followed" under a "storm of shells and minie balls," remembered one
North Carolina officer. "The enemy opened on us with infantry & artillery &
made the woods pretty hot." Despite the deluge of projectiles not one soldier
was wounded or killed in the abandonment of the bridge position. Quick acting
Federal skirmishers from the 63rd Indiana Infantry of Henderson's brigade
bolted across the remnants of the bridge, however, and managed to capture
about thirty men of the Confederate rear guard. The price was a small one to pay
for holding onto the position for so long, and the balance of Hagood's force
escaped in a hasty retreat up the Public Road. The Southerners halted two miles
from the creek in order to form a line of battle to cover Simonton's withdrawal.
Hagood had already abandoned his position at the church when a courier arrived
there with a report for him from Colonel Simonton: the Federals were extending
around Simonton's left and moving to attack. Simonton added that he could not
hold his position on the Telegraph Road much longer. The courier, however,
could not find Hagood and hurried back to Simonton with the distressing
news.[23]

Hagood soon had his troops in line to support the rear guard's retreat. The
general dispatched Capt. William E. Stoney of his staff, who had earlier been
with Simonton on the skirmish line at Cowan's, to tell Simonton to immediately
fall back. Stoney, together with a courier, galloped off and located the colonel
with his command in two wings on either side of the Telegraph Road, the right
wing under immediate threat of attack.

As soon as he received the message, Simonton ordered Lieutenant Rankin
to limber up his artillery, which had been firing into the Federals in his front,
and retreat with the infantry down a path through the swamp in their rear.
Rankin had managed to withdraw only one cannon several hundred yards when
the Federals suddenly attacked. The blue-clad troops came on so rapidly that

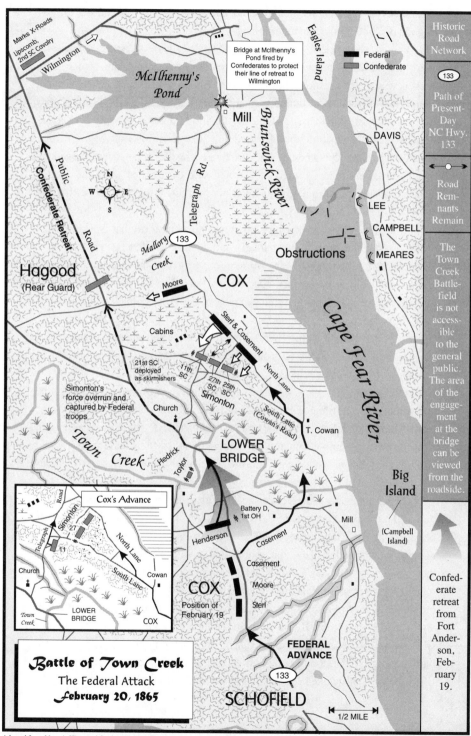

Marks X-Roads,
Lipscomb,
2nd SC Cavalry

Wilmington

McIlhenny's
Pond

Mill

Brunswick River

Eagles Island

Bridge at McIlhenny's
Pond fired by
Confederates to protect
their line of retreat to
Wilmington

Federal
Confederate

Historic
Road
Network

133

Path of
Present-
Day
NC Hwy.
133

DAVIS

LEE

CAMPBELL

MEARES

Obstructions

Road
Rem-
nants
Remain

Confederate Retreat

Public Road

Telegraph Rd.

Mallory Creek

133

Moore

COX

Cape Fear River

The
Town
Creek
Battle-
field
is not
access-
ible
to the
general
public.
The area
of the
engage-
ment
at the
bridge
can be
viewed
from the
roadside.

Hagood
(Rear Guard)

Cabins

Sterl & Casement

North Lane

21st SC
deployed
as skirmishers

11th
SC

27th 25th
SC SC
Simonton

South Lane
(Cowan's Road)

T. Cowan

Simonton's
force overrun and
captured by Federal
troops

Church

LOWER
BRIDGE

Big
Island

Town Creek

Hedrick

Taylor

Battery D,
1st OH

Mill

(Campbell
Island)

Cox's Advance

Road

Simonton

27

Telegraph

11

Church

Town
Creek

LOWER
BRIDGE

North Lane

South Lane

Cowan

COX

Henderson

Casement

COX

Position of
February 19

Casement

Moore

Sterl

FEDERAL
ADVANCE

133

SCHOFIELD

1/2 MILE

Confed-
erate
retreat
from
Fort
Ander-
son,
Febru-
ary
19.

Battle of Town Creek
The Federal Attack
February 20, 1865

Adapted from *Moore's Historical Guide to the Wilmington Campaign & the Battles for Fort Fisher* (Forthcoming from Savas Publishing)   Mark A. Moore

Simonton had little choice but to stand and fight. Stoney dashed off to alert Hagood of Simonton's desperate situation.[24]

With fixed bayonets, Casement's and Sterl's brigades attacked Simonton"s men "impetuously and with the wildest enthusiasm," according to one New York newspaper correspondent. The 3,000 troops cheered as they advanced, though it was a long and fatiguing charge across a field dotted with pine trees and scrub oaks. LeVant Dodge of the 177th Ohio Infantry of Casement's Second Brigade, Third Division, stumbled and fell just as the assault began, losing several large sweet potatoes he had discovered in the same cache foraged by South Carolina soldiers posted at Town Creek earlier that morning. Dodge picked himself up and quickly resumed his position in the battle line, but not without regrets for those lost yams.

The initial resistance met by Dodge and his comrades, that is, skirmishers of the 21st South Carolina and a small contingent of Confederate cavalry, were dispersed with relative ease. "The firing in our front became rapid and constant, and we could hear the enemy cheering as they drove in our skirmish line, through the pines," recalled Abram Clement of the 11th South Carolina. Most of these skirmishers never rejoined their comrades on the battle line, and were either captured or had simply fled—Simonton suspected the latter. But the remaining Southerners answered Union cheer with "rebel yell" and met the bayonet attack with galling volleys of small arms fire and artillery canister as the Northerners came into view. Lieutenant Rankin even unlimbered the cannon he had withdrawn and fired on the attacking Federals from his new position in the rear of Simonton's line. "By this time the balls were flying around at a great rate," observed Abram Clement. "The firing continued to increase until it was a perfect roar." So intense was the gunfire that sparks from discharged weapons ignited the field of sedge broom grass.[25]

The Confederates' destructive sheet of fire killed three and wounded thirty-one of the enemy. A lieutenant in the 12th Kentucky (U. S.) Infantry of Sterl's brigade witnessed the terrible result of a discharge by "St. Paul." He had demanded the surrender of the gun crew as it was in the act of firing. "If you fire that gun I will kill you," threatened the Kentuckian. "Kill and be damned," replied Sgt. Benjamin F. Hunter, commander of the howitzer, who turned and ordered a gunner to discharge the weapon. The artilleryman jerked the lanyard and a loud boom erupted. The long burst of barrel flame and cloudy burst of smoke was succeeded almost immediately by the thump-thump-thump of lead balls ripping into flesh and bone. An enormous rolling moan from the victims filled the broken wooded lot. The cannister had enfiladed Company H of the

Corporal Theodore J. Wagner
Company A, 23rd Michigan Infantry

Ellen and Dick McMann

104th Ohio Infantry at point-blank range, killing and wounding twenty soldiers—more than half the Union casualties in the fight. Federal soldiers instantly
cut down the gunner and pounced on Sergeant Hunter. They would have run
Hunter through with their bayonets had the lieutenant of the 12th Kentucky not
spared him, saying, "He's too brave a man to be killed."[26]

P. O. Phillips of the 65th Illinois Infantry claimed that he was the only
member of his regiment wounded, albeit slightly, in the assault at Town Creek.
A whizzing artillery shell fragment or lead ball caused a deep contusion of
Phillips' left thigh after glancing off his bayonet scabbard draped at his side.
Phillips' leg swelled up so quickly that he was unable to continue the advance.
"The missile striking my scabbard . . . probably saved my thigh from being torn
off enough to bleed me to death," Phillips later recalled, "but no bones were
broken and just enough blood flowed so that I could say 'I have bled for my
country as well as fought for her.'"[27]

Private William Reese of the 16th Kentucky (U. S.) Infantry of Sterl's
brigade was also wounded in the attack, but not by a Confederate projectile.
Reese, a 33-year old enlistee, injured himself with his own rifle-musket. As his
unit neared the Confederate line, Reese plummeted into a rifle pit he did not see
in the gathering darkness. As he fell, the butt of his gun smashed into his lower
abdomen, causing a hernia and severely bruising his testicles. Writhing in pain
in the sedgebroom grass that burned around him, Reese missed the rest of the
battle. It was the only wound Reese sustained during the war, and would cause
him some discomfort for the rest of his life.[28]

Meanwhile, Phillips' and Reese's comrades soon overwhelmed the Confederates, who were outnumbered about eight to one. Even so, Simonton's men
stood their ground until overpowered in hand-to-hand combat with Cox's
troops. At the head of the 65th Illinois Infantry of Casement's brigade as it
plowed into the enemy's line, William O'Leary grabbed a Confederate lieutenant by the throat and "told him that if he did not surrendered he would knock his
damned head off. He surrendered!" O'Leary later proudly exclaimed. The Irish-
man promptly confiscated the Southern officer's revolver, sword and field
glasses as souvenirs. "There was no running in these rebels," another Union
soldier marveled, "they held their ragged works until the guns were snatched out
of their hands."[29]

It is difficult to determine with any precision the exact Confederate casualties in this engagement, primarily because so few reports were filed or have
survived from this period of the war. Perhaps twenty Southerners were killed
and wounded in the action that ended as the sun disappeared behind the long

leaf pines. Among the casualties was a soldier named "Prince" of Company B, 11th South Carolina Infantry, who was shot in the face at point-blank range while fighting with his unit on the left of the line. The Union soldier who shot Prince was so close when he discharged his weapon that cartridge paper from the round protruded from the wound near Prince's mouth. Despite the close-quarter fighting, most of the Confederates survived the battle and were taken prisoner. In all, Cox's troops captured 375 officers and men, including Colonel Simonton, who personally surrendered his command to General Cox. Both pieces of Lieutenant Rankin's artillery and three battle flags were also captured.[30]

Among the prisoners were Privates John and James Nixon. Members of the Edenton Bell Battery, the Nixon brothers had enlisted together in Bertie County back in January, 1862. They both had fought and survived the battles of Fredericksburg, White Hall, and Goldsboro. For them the war was now over. Though captives, the Nixon brothers could take comfort in the notion that they had fought bravely and were together—alive.[31]

Instead of surrendering some Confederates chose to escape—or at least tried to escape—into the surrounding woods and swamps. The Federals pursued them until it was too dark to see and captured many, including Captain Wescoat and Abram Clement. As the Federals had poured over the Southern battle line and encircled the beleaguered defenders, Wescoat and Clement took off on what the latter described as "a race almost of life and death," with four Union soldiers right behind them, firing on the run. The South Carolinians eventually became winded, and had to stop, hiding in a clump of bushes. But the Federals, soldiers of the 12th Kentucky Infantry, were close behind and called out for their surrender. "We had nothing to do but give ourselves up," Clement lamented. The Kentuckians confiscated Wescoat's sword, sword belt, and pistol, and almost everything Clement had been carrying except a photograph and a lead pencil. They were then marched back to the battlefield and placed under guard with the rest of the prisoners.[32]

Like Clement and Wescoat, Sgt. William V. Izlar of Company G (Edisto Rifles), 25th South Carolina Infantry, attempted to escape the Federal tidal wave. When the battle ended, Izlar was on the far right of Simonton's line. He and several comrades realized the game was up and fled, hoping to make their way back to Hagood's main force. They struggled through the darkness and a dense swamp to reach the Public Road west of the Telegraph Road. As soon as the South Carolinians stepped onto the thoroughfare, however, they found themselves in the midst of Yankees from Henderson's brigade. "Hello, Johnnie," a Union soldier greeted Izlar, "how deep have you been in?" Disgusted with his

Sgt. William V. Izlar

Izlar, Edisto Rifles

bad luck, Izlar merely replied, "Just so deep," while holding his hand at the heighth of his waist. "I felt terribly chagrined," Izlar wrote, "but quiet submission was the only alternative."[33]

An undetermined number of Confederates managed to elude their would-be captors. One of them was General Hagood's staffer, Capt. William E. Stoney. Hagood had sent the officer back into the fray with direct orders for Simonton: "He must come," Hagood insisted. Simonton was to "throw away his artillery and make a run for it." Despite thrashing his mount at breakneck speed, Stoney arrived only in time to "see the overwhelming lines of the enemy sweep over

Simonton—the artillery firing till the enemy got within a few feet of it, and the infantry standing by the gun and resisting till overpowered hand to hand." The staff officer never reached Simonton. As he got sucked into the swirling melee, Stoney's horse was shot under him and he fell to the ground. Unhurt, Stoney managed to scramble away, though he was unable to rejoin his command for several days.[34]

Johnson Hagood feared the worst. The fighting had long since ended and yet neither Simonton nor Stoney had reported to him. What little news he received, and all of it was bad, reached his ears from the few stragglers from Simonton's rout able to stumble their way through the boggy terrain and rejoin their commands. Their testimony was proof enough. Hagood ordered a general retreat to Wilmington. Hagood accommodated the stragglers by taking up a temporary position behind Mallory Creek, keeping a strong skirmish line in his front with a squad of cavalry patrolling the environs.

About half of Lipscomb's South Carolina Cavalry formed the rear guard for Hagood's haggard column of marchers, while the balance was thrown forward to guard the position at McIlhenny's Mill. Hagood rode ahead of his men and reached the city about 8:30 that evening, February 20. Decimated and dejected, the infantry and artillery crossed over the Brunswick River pontoon bridge and by steam ferry over the Cape Fear River three hours later. After burning the pontoons the cavalry left a small picket force on Eagles Island. Initially, Hagood's troops were ordered to reinforce Hoke's Brigades at the Forks Road entrenchments, but those orders were soon countermanded and they were sent to encamp at Hilton, on the northern outskirts of the city.[35]

Hindered by the dense swamp and encroaching darkness, Col. Orlando Moore's brigade failed to intercept Hagood's fleeing soldiers. The escape of the enemy compelled the brigade commander to retrace his steps and rejoin Cox, who had bivouacked his troops on the Telegraph Road battlefield. Confederate prisoners from the engagement were rounded up and placed under a heavy guard for the night, while the dead, both blue and gray, remained where they had gone down. The dark night and severe fatigue brought on by the day's constant marching and fighting delayed the battle's survivors from burying the dead until first light the following morning. In the meantime, Cox's and Simonton's veterans slept soundly among the prostrated bodies of their "silent comrades" dotting the bloodied ground. One Union soldier noted that "in a few hours everything was quiet as if no din of battle had ever been there." Federal engineers, meanwhile, spent the evening repairing the bridge to enable the Ohio artillery and the bulk of

Henderson's brigade, which had fought all day at the lower bridge, to cross and reunite with Cox.[36]

Why had the Confederate defensive position at Town Creek unravelled so quickly? The blame must fall on Johnson Hagood, who allowed Jacob Cox to outflank him with impunity. Hagood was not about to accept blame for the defeat, however, and fingered Robert Hoke and Charles Simonton as the culprits for the fiasco. The South Carolinian impugned Hoke's generalship by questioning the exigency for attempting to hold Town Creek line. "The propriety of making the obstinate stand at Town Creek at all," Hagood wrote, "rests with the direction of affairs." In that deftly-drafted sentence of just eighteen words, Hagood relieved himself of responsibility, took credit for Simonton's resolute stand—and impaled Hoke. He twisted the blade of his pen once more by adding, "It delayed the evacuation of Wilmington but little and was a hazardous adventure."

As disparaging as he was toward Hoke, Hagood saved most of his venom for Charles Simonton. He blamed the colonel, a commander with but limited field experience, for disobeying orders and allowing himself to be coerced into battle. "His fault," censured Hagood, "was in allowing his greatly inferior force to become engaged in a line of battle behind obstructions rapidly thrown up, when the occasion required him, and he had been directed [by Hagood], to make an obstinate skirmish fight." In a postscript to this criticism, Hagood added, "For this the country was admirably suited." After heaping additional condemnations upon Simonton, even Hagood was compelled to concede that his troops "behaved with the accustomed gallantry," and their "obstinate defense of the flank" saved Hagood's command. In a final parting discharge that damned Simonton with faint praise, Hagood noted that the colonel's "errors certainly leaned to virtue's side." Unfortunately, Hagood's fast and loose rendition of Simonton's supposed field foibles conveniently ignored several critical points. Colonel Simonton had but 400-500 men to throw across a broad front into the face of an aggressive veteran enemy force outnumbering him about eight to one. In addition, Hagood requested that Simonton concurrently execute several arguably incompatible tactical feats, including the rapid extension of his line to the left to cover two roads, and the placement of a "reserve" behind each flank. Given that Simonton himself did not believe his force large enough to adequately guard both points, Hagood's order to spread his men and pull enough soldiers out of line to form two reserves—while in direct contact with Cox's Federals—made little sense. Most significantly, Hagood had ordered Simonton to "close his reserves together" to meet the enemy when he reached the Telegraph Road; that is, to consolidate into a battle line. In the end, Hagood's criticisms make him look petty and small.[37]

While Johnson Hagood may have been pleased with his escape from the Town Creek line, the evacuation provided small comfort to General Hoke. The North Carolinia officer had realized for some time that if Hagood was defeated at Town Creek, Wilmington's doom was sealed, for nothing could stop Jacob Cox from marching within range of the city. As Hoke feared, by mid-afternoon on February 21, Cox's pursuing brigades reached the west bank of the Brunswick River within sight of Wilmington's skyline. Soon thereafter, Union skirmishers pushed across Eagles Island headed toward the city, while Cox's artillery commenced a long-range, if short-lived duel with Hagood's cannon along the banks of the Cape Fear River.

Hoke made hurried preparations to evacuate the city. Before sunrise the following day, February 22, Hoke's despondent Southern army moved northward toward Goldsboro to assemble with the remnants of other scattered commands. As the soldiers trudged through Wilmington's dark streets a deathlike stillness surrounded them. "Lights could be seen from but few windows," observed one Confederate, "and these appeared to be the last rays of departing hope."[38]

Dashing the "departing hope" of the beleaguered Confederacy, Federal troops entered Wilmington later that morning. As Grant and Sherman had hoped, the Union capture of the city had a direct influence on Sherman's operations, providing him with both a safe haven along the Carolina coast and a base of supply. The troops that soon reinforced Sherman through Wilmington gave him an army not only capable of contesting any threat inside the Old North State, but strong enough to threaten the state capital of Raleigh, as well as Robert E. Lee in Virginia. With Grant in his front and Sherman poised to attack his rear, Lee had little choice but to evacuate the Richmond-Petersburg line and move to join forces with Joe Johnston in North Carolina. Grant caught up with Lee and forced his surrender at Appomattox Courthouse, only six weeks after Wilmington's fall. Jacob Cox's victory at Town Creek and the subsequent capture of Wilmington did not end the Confederacy, but they hastened its downfall.

Notes

1. Grant to Sherman, March 16, 1865, *OR* 47, pt. 2, 859.

2. Hagood to Anderson, February 19, 1865, U.S. War Department, *The War of the Rebellion: The Official Records of the Union and Confederate Armies*, 128 vols. (Wash-

ington, D.C., 1880-1901), series I, vol. 47, pt. 2, 1228. Hereinafter cited as *OR*. All references are to series I unless otherwise noted; Johnson Hagood, *Memoirs of the War of Secession* (Columbia, 1910), 342; William Calder Diary, February 19, 1865, Perkins Library, Duke University, Durham, North Carolina. According to military accounts, the Confederate earthworks at Town Creek contained "a Whitworth rifled cannon and two brass smoothbore twelve pounder field pieces." Jacob Dolson Cox, *Campaigns of the Civil War: March to the Sea* (Franklin and Nashville), 150; Report of Jacob D. Cox, May 15, 1865, *OR* 47, pt. 1, 961; Hagood's earthworks, since pushed down, stood on a bluff on the north bank of Town Creek just west of present-day Highway 133 at Town Creek bridge. Hagood to Anderson, February 19, 1865, *OR* 47, pt. 2, 1228.

3. Hagood, *Memoirs of the War of Secession*, 342.

4. Report of Jacob D Cox, May 15, 1865, *OR* 47, pt. 1, 961; Cox, *March to the Sea*, 150; Hagood, *Memoirs of the War of Secession*, 340-341; James Sprunt, *Chronicles of the Cape Fear River 1660-1916* (Raleigh, 1916), map, 412; *OR* Atlas, CV, 8.

5. Slann L. C. Simmons, "Diary of Abram W. Clement, 1865," *South Carolina Historical Magazine* LIX, 2 (April, 1958), 79. Hereinafter cited as Simmons, "Diary of Abram W. Clement."

6. Hagood, *Memoirs of the War of Secession*, 342 Report of Jacob D. Cox, May 15, 1865, *OR* 47, pt. 2, 961; Report of Thomas J. Henderson, April 6, 1865, Ibid., pt. 1, 969; Cox, *March to the Sea*, 150; B. F. Thompson, *History of the 112th Regiment of Illinois Volunteer Infantry in the Great War of the Rebellion 1862-1865* (Toulan, 1885), 305; Cox to Campbell, February 19, 1865, *OR* 47, pt. 2, 495; Report of Oscar W. Sterl, April 28, 1865, Ibid., pt. 1, 965.

7. Hagood, *Memoirs of the War of Secession*, 342.

8. William Calder Diary, February 19, 1865, Perkins Library; Campbell to Cox, February 19, 1865, *OR* 47, pt. 2, 496.

9. Report of Thomas J. Henderson, April 6, 1865, *OR* 47, pt. 1, 969; Thompson, *History of the 112th Illinois Infantry*, 305; Cox to Campbell, February 19, 1865, *OR* 47, pt. 2, 495; Report of Jacob D. Cox, May 15, 1865, Ibid., pt. 1, 961; Campbell to Cox, February 19, 1865, Ibid., pt. 2, 496.

10. Report of Jacob D. Cox, May 15, 1865, *OR* 47, pt. 1, 961; Report of John S. Casement, April 9, 1865, Ibid., 968; Report of Oscar W. Sterl, April 28, 1865, Ibid., 965; Thompson, *History of the 112th Illinois Infantry*, 306; W. S. Thurstin, *History One Hundred and Eleventh Regiment Ohio Volunteer Infantry* (Toledo, 1894), 118; Cox to Schofield, February 20, 1865, *OR* 47, pt. 2, 509; Oliver S. Spaulding Diary, February 20, 1865, Library of Congress; "A Memory," *National Tribune*, February 4, 1915.

11. Cox, *March to the Sea*, 151; Report of Thomas J. Henderson, April 6, 1865, *OR* 47, pt. 1, p969-970; Hagood, *Memoirs of the War of Secession*, 342; William Calder Diary, February 20, 1865, Perkins Library.

12. Hagood, *Memoirs of the War of Secession*, p342-343; Hardee to Bragg, February 20, 1865, *OR* 47, pt. 2, 1231; Hoke to Hardee, February 20, 1865, Ibid., 1233; Hoke to Lee, February 20, 1865, Ibid., 1233.

13. Report of Jacob D. Cox, May 15, 1865, *OR* 47, pt. 1, 962; Report of John S. Casement, April 9, 1865, Ibid., 968. Report of Oscar W. Sterl, April 28, 1865, Ibid., 965. Thomas Speed to Parents, February 25, 1865, Thomas Speed Collection, Filson Club, Louisville, Kentucky.

14. Simmons, "Diary of Abram W. Clement," 79-80. The Confederate vedettes were probably surprised and captured by soldiers of Cox's division who were crossing the creek on the morning of February 20. According to one Southern account, however, the pickets were taken captive not by Union infantry, but by a shore party of marines from the gunboats in the Cape Fear River. Charles Henry Simonton, "Circumstances of the Capture of Hagood's Brigade on 20th Feb'y 1865 at Cowan's Place on Town Creek near Wilmington, N. C.," 5, George Hall Moffett Papers, South Carolina Historical Society, Charleston. Hereinafter cited as Simonton, "Capture of Hagood's Brigade at Town Creek," Moffett Papers.

15. Simonton, "Capture of Hagood's Brigade at Town Creek," Moffett Papers, 1. Hagood, *Memoirs of the War of Secession*, 343; William V. Izlar, *A Sketch of the War Record of the Edisto Rifles, 1861-1865* (Columbia, 1914), 115.

16. Hagood, *Memoirs of the War of Secession*, map, 341.

17. Simonton, "Capture of Hagood's Brigade at Town Creek," Moffett Papers, p1-2.

18. Hagood, *Memoirs of the War of Secession*, 344-345; Simonton, "Capture of Hagood's Brigade at Town Creek," Moffett Papers, 2; Hagood to Parker, February 20, 1865, *OR* 47, pt. 2, 1236.

19. Report of Jacob D. Cox, May 15, 1865, *OR* 47, pt. 1, 962; Report of John S. Casement, April 9, 1865, Ibid., 968; Report of Oscar W. Sterl, April 28, 1865, Ibid., 965.

20. Simonton, "Capture of Hagood's Brigade at Town Creek," , Moffett Papers, 3. Hagood, *Memoirs of the War of Secession*, 344; Izlar, *Edisto Rifles*, 116.

21. Richard Dillard, *The Civil War in Chowan County*, (n.p., 1916), 5-7.

22. Report of Jacob D. Cox, May 15, 1865, *OR*, 47, pt. 1, 962; Cox to Schofield, February 20, 1865, Ibid., pt. 2, 509; *New York Herald*, February 27, 1865.

23. William Calder Diary, February 20, 1865, Perkins Library; Zaccheus Ellis to Mother, March 1, 1865, Zaccheus Ellis Papers, Southern Historical Collection, University of North Carolina at Chapel Hill; Report of Thomas Henderson, April 6, 1865, *OR* 47, pt. 1, 970; Hagood, *Memoirs of the War of Secession*, 345-346; Simonton, "Capture of Hagood's Brigade at Town Creek," Moffett Papers, 3.

24. Hagood, *Memoirs of the War of Secession*, 345-346; "Captain William E. Stoney," *Confederate Veteran*, vol. 4, 383.

25. *New York Herald*, February 27, 1865; See also: Thomas Speed to Parents, February 25, 1865, Speed Collection, Filson Club; LeVant Dodge, "A Memory," *National Tribune*, February 4, 1915; Simmons, "Diary of Abram W. Clement," 80.

26. General Cox lost about thirty men in the charge at Town Creek; Report of Jacob D. Cox, May 15, 1865, *OR* 47, pt. 1, 964; Cox to Schofield, February 20, 1865, Ibid., pt. 2, 509; Colonel Oscar W. Sterl noted that the Federal loss in the attack was three killed and thirty-one wounded; Report of Oscar W. Sterl, April 28, 1865, Ibid., pt. 1, 966;

According to one of only four Confederate accounts of the Town Creek battle uncovered so far, Sergeant Hunter ordered Pvt. William H. Hassell to fire "St. Paul" at the attacking Union troops, despite the threat against him by the lieutenant of the 12th Kentucky U.S. Infantry. If Hassell was the gunner who jerked the lanyard, he miraculously escaped capture. According to military records, Private Hassell was paroled with his unit—Company B, 3rd Battalion N. C. Light Artillery—in Greensboro on April 28, 1865; Dillard, "The Civil War in Chowan County," 6-7; Louis Manarin, *North Carolina Troops 1861-1865: A Roster*, 13 vols. (Raleigh, 1966-1993), vol. 1, 351. For a Union account of the incident see: James R. Bentley, ed., "The Civil War Memoirs of Captain Thomas Speed," *Filson Club History Quarterly,* 44 (July, 1970), 266-267.

27. O. Phillips to Ruth Phillips, February 20, 1914, Brunswick Town and Fort Anderson State Historic Site, Winnabow, North Carolina.

28. Declaration for Original Invalid Pension for William Reese, June 20, 1884, copy in possession of Timothy J. Reese, Burkittsville, Maryland.

29. O. Phillips to Ruth Phillips, February 20, 1914, Brunswick Town and Fort Anderson State Historic Site, Winnabow, North Carolina.

30. Thomas Speed to Parents, February 25, 1865, Speed Collection, Filson Club; Simmons, "Diary of Abram W. Clement," 81; General Hagood wrote after the war that Colonel Simonton reported 330 South Carolina soldiers and officers captured by the Federals at Town Creek (perhaps twenty or thirty North Carolina artillerymen were also taken prisoner). Hagood figured that Simonton lost twenty soldiers killed, and 100 escaped, but "coming out of the route and not finding the brigade that night, straggled off to South Carolina, and were no more, with very few exceptions, heard of in the war." Hagood, *Memoirs of the War of Secession*, 347. In a 1904 account of the Town Creek battle, Charles H. Simonton noted the "whole capture" from Hagood's Brigade consisted of twenty-seven officers, ninety soldiers of the 11th South Carolina Infantry, forty-five men of the 25th South Carolina Infantry, and 150 of the 27th South Carolina Infantry; Simonton, "Capture of Hagood's Brigade at Town Creek," Moffett Papers. Simonton's figures do not, however, account for the losses of the 21st South Carolina Infantry; See also: Report of Jacob D. Cox, May 15, 1865, *OR* 47, pt. 1, 963; Cox to Schofield, February 20, 1865, Ibid., pt. 2, 509; Report of Oscar W. Sterl, April 28, 1865, Ibid., pt. 1, p965-966; *New York Herald*, February 27, 1865.

31. Manarin, *North Carolina Troops*, vol. 1, 354.

32. Simmons, "Diary of Abram W. Clement," 81.

33. Izlar, *Edisto Rifles*, 116-117.

34. Hagood, *Memoirs of the War of Secession*, 346; "Captain William E. Stoney," *Confederate Veteran*, vol. 4, 383.

35. Hagood to Anderson, February 20, 1865, *OR* 47, pt. 2, 1,236; Hagood, *Memoirs of the War of Secession*, 346; Zaccheus Ellis to Mother, March 1, 1865, Zaccheus Ellis Papers, Southern Historical Collection. William Calder Diary, February 20, 1865, Perkins Library.

36. Thomas Speed to Parents, February 25, 1865, Speed Collection, Filson Club.

37. "[Simonton's] fault was in allowing a greatly inferior force to become engaged in a line of battle behind obstructions hastily thrown up, when the occasion required him, and he had been directed, to make an obstinate skirmish fight," Hagood maintained. "Again when ordered to withdraw, instead of facing the rear and withdrawing. . .at a double quick. . .he endeavored to make a flank march along the enemy's front, with a view of getting a road down which to retire in column." Hagood, *Memoirs of the War of Secession*, 346-348.

38. *Fayetteville Observer Semi-Weekly*, March 2, 1865.

"It was a remarkable, if not decisive performance."

BATTLE IN THE SWAMP

William Cogswell's Brigade at the Battle of Averasboro

James S. Pula

A long the dusty North Carolina roads they trudged, their blue uniforms long ago dulled by the sun, the dirt, and the rain of months in the field. They were a veteran group, most of whom had been in the service since 1862. Many saw their first action in the Shenandoah Valley under John C. Fremont and in the Second Bull Run Campaign under John Pope. Five regiments fought at Chancellorsville and Gettysburg with the Eleventh Corps, following its crescent badge west to serve with distinction at Wauhatchie, Lookout Mountain, and in the Chattanooga and Knoxville campaigns. Then, when Ulysses S. Grant assumed overall command of the Federal armies, his replacement in the west, William T. Sherman, consolidated the Eleventh Corps with the Twelfth into the new Twentieth Corps. In the realignment, the five Eleventh Corps regiments, along with another regiment from the Twelfth Corps, were assigned to the new Third Brigade, Third Division, Twentieth Corps. Under this designation they fought gallantly during Sherman's Atlanta campaign, earning praise for their conduct at Rocky Face Ridge, Resaca, Kolb's Farm, Golgotha Church, Kenesaw Mountain, and Peach Tree Creek.[1] With the eventual surrender of Altanta, the brigade continued its march under Sherman to Savannah, then north into the Carolinas.

On January 16, 1865, command of the brigade passed to Col. William Cogswell. A native of Massachusetts, Cogswell was born into a well-to-do family that provided him with the best education available at the prestigious Phillips Andover Academy, Dartmouth College, and Harvard Law School. An attorney in Salem when the war erupted, his patriotism led him to enlist early in the 2nd Massachusetts. He came to his first brigade command as an unknown to those he would lead. Before the campaign ended, a veteran officer in the brigade would describe him as a "very attentive" officer who "strictly forbids all wanton destruction of private property. I think he is by far the best officer we have had at the head of this brigade."[2]

The troops Cogswell would lead through the Carolinas included six regiments from five states, evenly divided between Easterners and Westerners. The 55th and 73rd Ohio were raised at Norwalk and Chillicothe, respectively, in January 1862 and December 1861. After their first action in the mountains of West Vir-

Col. William Cogswell

USAMI

ginia, the two regiments served under Fremont in the Shenandoah Valley and with Pope during the Second Bull Run Campaign, earning reputations as solid fighting units. Joining the Eleventh Corps when it was created in the fall of 1862, they shared in the disaster at Chancellorsville, serving with honor both there and in the victory at Gettysburg before moving west. At Wauhatchie, Tennessee, the 73rd Ohio, along with the 33rd Massachusetts, also a member of Cogswell's Brigade, carried by storm a Confederate entrenchment on a hill in what Gen. U. S. Grant called "one of the most daring feats of arms of the war." Following the campaigns in Tennessee, the 55th and 73rd Ohio went on to play important roles in the victories of Sherman's marches to Atlanta and the sea. For the campaign through the Carolinas the 55th was led by Lt. Col. Edwin H. Powers and the 73rd by Lt. Col. Samuel H. Hurst.[3]

The other western regiment with Cogswell was the 26th Wisconsin, a German outfit raised in Milwaukee and the surrounding counties that won praise for its steadfast service at Chancellorsville, Gettysburg, Resaca, and Peach Tree Creek. Led by Lt. Col. Frederick C. Winkler, a Milwaukee lawyer, the regiment had been singled out for praise by the former brigade commander for its heroic stand at Peach Tree Creek, where it plugged a hole in the Union line against superior Confederate forces, capturing the colors of the 33rd Mississippi Infantry, killing its colonel, and decimating the rank and file. Always in the thick of the fray, when the final butcher's toll was compiled at the end of the war, "The

Sigel Regiment," as it was known, would rank fifth among all Federal infantry regiments in the percentage of men killed as a result of enemy action.[4] In fact, all three of the western regiments in Cogswell's brigade would be listed among the top "300 fighting regiments" identified by William F. Fox in his outstanding statistical work *Regimental Losses in the American Civil War, 1861-1865.*

Lt. Col. Frederick C. Winkler

Author's Collection

Among the Easterners, the 136th New York mustered in at Portage, New York, in September 1862. Serving at Chancellorsville and Gettysburg with the Eleventh Corps, the 136th was lucky enough to be in reserve or on the periphery in most of the corps' actions, taking heavy casualties only during Sherman's campaign to Atlanta. The regiment was now under Maj. Henry L. Arnold. The 33rd Massachusetts entered service at Springfield in August 1862. Known for having what was widely considered the best band in the Twentieth Corps, it, too, had seen its hottest action under Sherman, moving into the Carolinas under Lt. Col. Elisha Doane. The 20th Connecticut was the only regiment in Cogswell's brigade that could not trace its previous service to the Eleventh Corps. Organized at New Haven in September 1862, it served with the Twelfth Corps from Chancellorsville through the Chattanooga and Knoxville campaigns before moving south with Sherman through

Georgia as part of the Twentieth Corps. Lt. Col. Philo B. Buckingham of Seymour, Connecticut, led the regiment in the spring of 1865.[5]

For the coming campaign through the Carolinas, Sherman divided his forces into two wings. Each would move north within general supporting distance of the other. By doing so, Sherman was able to cut a wider swath through the seat of the rebellion, forage over a greater area to support his army, and force the Confederates to disperse their meager forces to guard various potential avenues of advance. The Right Wing under Maj. Gen. Oliver Otis Howard included the Fifteenth and Seventeenth Corps, while the Left Wing under Maj. Gen. Henry W. Slocum comprised the Fourteenth and Twentieth Corps. William Cogswell's brigade, numbering 88 officers and 1,399 men at the beginning of the Carolina Campaign, was designated the Third Brigade, Third Division, Twentieth Corps, under the division command of Maj. Gen. William T. Ward.[6]

On February 11, 1865, Cogswell's brigade waded the Big Salkehatchie River, pushing north toward Columbia, South Carolina. All along the route of march, Confederate irregulars looked on, unable to mount serious opposition to the methodical and powerful Union advance. From Columbia the column turned northwestward as Sherman pursued Confederates concentrating near the town of Cheraw. Although the movement was slowed by muddy roads, the men plodded on, crossing the Saluda River on a pontoon bridge at Mount Zion Church on the 18th. The soldiers turned northeast, the seemingly effortless rhythm of their fluid marching step marking them as veterans of many campaigns. They crossed the Broad River on the 20th, then pushed on through Winnsboro to Rocky Mount on the Catawba River on the 21st, marching across the Broad River once again on pontoons the following evening. All along the way Sherman's men sought out anything that could support the Confederate war effort, destroying cotton, crops, railroads, government buildings, warehouses, trains, wagons, and anything else of possible use to the enemy.[7]

Crossing the Wateree River on the 23rd, the column pushed on through Russell's Cross Roads to Hanging Rock on the 26th, crossed Little Lynch's Creek and Black Creek, finally arriving at Chesterfield Court House about 4:00 p.m. on March 3.[8] By this time the campaign through the Carolinas had already lasted longer than the march through Georgia from Atlanta to the sea. The men were tired, but victory was a strong antidote for their weariness, and everyone sensed victory in the air. Pressing on to Westfield Creek, the column camped at Grady's farm for the night, reaching Cheraw the following day only to find that Lt. Gen. William Hardee's Confederates had once again retired before the Northern advance, retreating all the way into North Carolina.[9] To many, it seemed the Confederates had lost either their means or their will to resist—perhaps both.[10]

By Sunday, March 5, Cogswell's brigade lay "quietly" in its camp west of the Great Pee Dee River near the boundary line between the two Carolinas. Throughout the campaign foragers actively scoured the countryside to provide men and horses with sustenance. In the month between February 4 and March 4, for example, Lt. Col. Winkler of the 26th Wisconsin estimated that foragers from his regiment alone brought in 800 pounds of wheat flour, 4,000 pounds of corn meal, 550 bushels of sweet potatoes, 13,000 pounds of meat, 900 pounds of lard, 150 pounds of dried fruit, and 1,200 bushels of corn for animal fodder. They also destroyed about 300 bales of cotton. As successful as they were, however, the foragers were not immune from danger. While out on an expedition between Cheraw and Seedsville on March 5, Capt. August Bartsch and ten men were "engaged in grinding corn at a mill" when they were approached by a cavalry force dressed in Union blue. They discovered the Southern subterfuge too late and all were taken prisoner, condemned to spend the balance of the war in Rebel prisons. But the fate of other foragers was worse. Some were murdered, hung along the roadside by local guerillas with signs around their necks reading "Death To Foragers."[11]

Despite the occasional loss of these men, spirits remained high. The brigade met little resistance on the march from Atlanta to the sea, and even less during its trek through the seat of the rebellion in South Carolina. To veterans unaccustomed to such little opposition, the ease with which the Federal army penetrated the hotbed of secession could mean only one thing: Southern resources had been exhausted and the war was winding down. Everywhere, it seemed, the news was good, the Confederates were on the run, and no serious resistance was anticipated. "I see the northern papers predict a great battle," wrote Lt. Col. Winkler. "I doubt it. Our numbers will be so imposing that prudence will advise the Confederates to retreat."[12]

Several miles to the north, where the Confederate forces were concentrating, Gen. Joseph E. Johnston had other ideas. Hampered by a lack of railroad equipment, poor roads, and other obstacles, Johnston nevertheless determined to concentrate all available forces at Fayetteville, North Carolina, in the hope of arresting Sherman's progress. Establishing his headquarters at Raleigh, the Confederate commander feared the loss of that city would disrupt supplies to Robert E. Lee's besieged army in Virginia. Thus, he determined to attack Sherman while the two wings of the Union army remained separated, hoping to defeat one wing before it could be supported by the other, and in that way force

Sherman to halt his relentless march or possibly even retire. To this end, he ordered Hardee to select a promising defensive position from which to contest the advance of Slocum's wing before it could be supported by the rest of Sherman's army.[13]

Cogswell's brigade left its camp on March 6, marched through Cheraw that evening, and crossed the Great Pee Dee River on pontoons about 3:00 a.m. Advancing into the Tarheel State, the column marched through intermittent rain storms over "bad roads," fording several streams including the Lumber River and Rockfish Creek in the process. As they trudged along the narrow dirt roads, their attention fell on a crudely marked sign inscribed "fift 3 mils to Fatville." The wording convinced Adin B. Underwood in the 33rd Massachusetts that "phonetic reform in spelling had broken out early here." The column reached the Cape Fear River near "Fatville," or more popularly represented on the maps as "Fayetteville," on March 11. Once again the Confederates were forced to withdraw before the omposing Union host.[14]

On Sunday, March 12, the men rested and attended church services. The next day they passed in review through Fayetteville before crossing the Cape Fear River on pontoons. Lt. Col. Winkler found Fayetteville "a fine place, as large as Savannah. The arsenal was broken down, as it was apprehended that burning it might endanger adjacent buildings." Unlike the treatment meted out to their neighbors to the south, "Orders have said that the people of North Carolina are not to be treated like enemies; nothing but necessary stores are to be taken, and no ruthless burning, etc. will be tolerated. I fear it will not be found easy to enforce this order."[15]

On the 14th Colonel Cogswell led the 20th Connecticut, 33rd Massachusetts, and 102nd Illinois—the latter from the Second Brigade—on a reconnaissance mission north along the Goldsboro Road across Silver Run Creek to the Black (or South) River. At the same time, Lt. Col. Samuel H. Hurst of 73rd Ohio led the rest of Cogswell's Brigade—the 73rd and 55th Ohio, 26th Wisconsin, and 136th New York—east along the Tarborough Road to Great Creek on the Goldsboro Road near Black River. Arriving at Silver Run Creek without opposition, Cogswell left a force on guard there and rode over to Hurst's column just in time to encounter a small force of Southern cavalry along Evon Creek near the Black River. Cogswell deployed five companies of the 55th Ohio as skirmishers, sparking a "hot fire for twenty minutes" before the Buckeyes drove the enemy across the river. The retrograde movement uncovered a strong force of Confederates on the far bank. Roused to action, enemy artillery opened on Cogswell's men from four separate pieces, signifying the presence of a large enemy force the general estimated as brigade strength. The reconnaissance successfully completed and the enemy position uncovered, Cogswell retraced his path back to camp, arriving after dark following a round-trip of some twenty-two miles. The information cost the lives of two men from the 55th Ohio.[16]

Ahead of Cogswell's men, Hardee's Confederate corps spent the day feverishly digging in south of Averasboro to intercept the advance of the Twentieth Corps. Sherman, meanwhile, left Fayetteville on the 15th and guided his army in three columns. Slocum held the left or northern flank and headed for Smithfield before turning east toward Bentonville. The Fifteenth Corps formed the middle column, and Howard's force comprised the right or southern wing. Hardee hoped to bring Slocum's column to grief before it could be supported by the other two.[17]

Cogswell's Brigade marched out of Fayetteville along the Raleigh Plank Road at 6:30 a.m. on the morning of March 15, covering fourteen miles through what Underwood described as "cherry trees in blossom, elms and maples in leaf." The men labored along the slick roads throughout the morning and afternoon before halting to make camp at 5:00 p.m. between Silver Run and Taylor's Hole Creek. While they marched, Maj. Gen. Judson Kilpatrick's Federal cavalry encountered Lt. Gen. Joseph Wheeler's Confederate horsemen guarding the road to Raleigh. Pushing the Southerners back, Kilpatrick's troopers ran into Maj. Gen. William B. Taliaferro's Confederate infantry division, which sparked a sharp fight amidst the wooded marshes about six miles south of Averasboro. Hard- pressed by the larger Rebel force, Kilpatrick dug in behind hastily constructed breastworks to await the arrival of supporting infantry. William Hardee, in overall command of the Confederate force there, launched several sharp probes against the makeshift line, but the dismounted Union cavalry held until the arrival of Gen. William Hawley's brigade, the advance of the Twentieth Corps infantry.[18]

In the early morning fog of the 16th, Kilpatrick and Hawley pushed their men forward over the soft ground in search of the enemy. About a mile beyond Taylor's Hole Creek the Rebels suddenly appeared, smashing into the Federal advance in a furious charge that stunned Hawley's men and threatened to turn his flanks. Though the situation was desperate, Hawley's mixed-state brigade fought stubbornly and was able to hold out against attempts to overrun his position.[19]

Back in the Twentieth Corps camps, Cogswell's regiments marched at 6:30 a.m. the same morning, assigned with the rest of Ward's division to repair the road that Maj. Gen. Alpheus Williams found to be "literally impassable without corduroying."[20] About 7:30 a.m., as they were busily attending their task, William received word that Kilpatrick and Hawley had run into a strong enemy force. Reacting quickly to the danger, he ordered Ward's division forward to relieve Hawley's hard-pressed men. In the lead, Cogswell's brigade covered about five miles over what Winkler termed "difficult and muddy roads" before crossing Taylor's Hole Creek. A mile beyond the stream the sounds of combat became unmistakably clear.[21] To the veterans of so many hard-fought fields, the rapid rattle of musketry echoing sharply back along the column meant only one thing: the war they had been fighting for so long and which appeared to be winding down was, just ahead, heating up again. The jaunty unopposed march through the Carolinas was over. They would have to face yet another trial by fire before they could entertain any hope of seeing their homes and loved ones again.

If William Hardee had anything to do with it, the battle he was planning would prolong the war his enemy believed was nearly over. "Old Reliable," as he was known by his men, located his defenses skillfully along a ridge in a narrow neck of land between two rivers and fronted by a swampy area. His right flank rested near the Cape Fear River, while his left was anchored amid marshy lands along the Black River. The intervening line protected the junction of the Raleigh and Goldsboro roads. In the foremost line he placed Taliaferro's 4,500-man division. These troops were the least experienced Confederates on the field. The division consisted of two brigades of converted heavy artillerists from South Carolina and Georgia taken from the garrisons about Charleston and commanded by Brig. Gen. Stephen Elliott, Jr., and Col. Alfred Rhett. These rookie infantrymen were placed across the Fayetteville-Raleigh Road facing south with orders to hold as long as possible and then fall back on a second line of entrenchments 300 yards behind the first. Still farther back, in a third line constructed more formidably than the first two and located some 600 yards from the second line, Hardee placed the larger division of Maj. Gen. Lafayette McLaws. These six infantry brigades, together with two brigades of Gen. Joseph Wheeler's mounted troops, gave Hardee a total strength of about 11,000 men deployed across a narrow but deep front. The position, according to the historian of the Army of the Cumberland, "was not strong, except from entrenchments and the softness of the ground before it, which scarcely admitted the deployment and advance of infantry, and rendered the movement of horses almost impossible."[22]

Despite the condition of the ground, General Williams determined to press forward with a probing attack on Hardee's position. Ward's division, leading the advance, deployed about 9:30 a.m., with Col. Henry Case's First Brigade going into line on the left of the Raleigh Road, Cogswell's Third Brigade straddling the

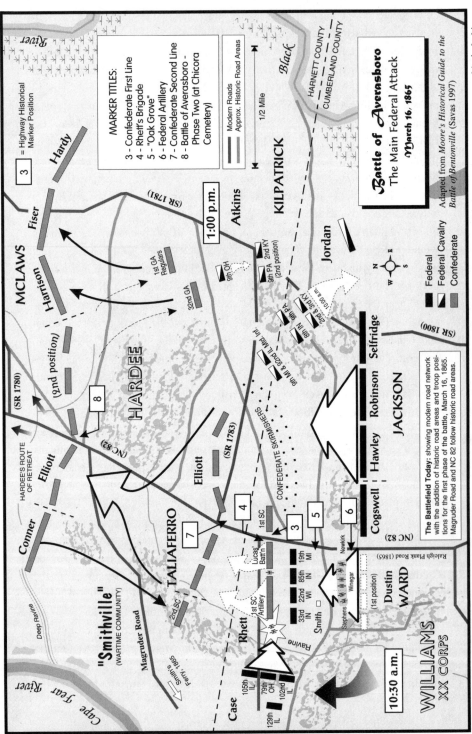

Mark A. Moore

Battle of Averasboro
The Main Federal Attack
March 16, 1865

Adapted from *Moore's Historical Guide to the Battle of Bentonville* (Savas 1997)

MARKER TITLES:
3 - Confederate First Line
4 - Rhett's Brigade
5 - "Oak Grove"
6 - Federal Artillery
7 - Confederate Second Line
8 - Battle of Averasboro - Phase Two (at Chicora Cemetery)

Modern Roads
Approx. Historic Road Areas

3 = Highway Historical Marker Position

1/2 Mile

Federal
Federal Cavalry
Confederate

The Battlefield Today: showing modern road network with the addition of historic road areas and troop positions for the first phase of the battle, March 16, 1865. Magruder Road and NC 82 follow historic road areas.

HARNETT COUNTY
CUMBERLAND COUNTY

Black River

KILPATRICK

Atkins

1:00 p.m.

Jordan

Selfridge

Robinson

JACKSON

Hawley

Cogswell

Newkirk

Raleigh Plank Road (1865)

WARD

Dustin

Winegar

Stephens

(1st position)

Smith

2nd & 3rd KY

8th IN

9th IN & 92nd IL Mtd. Inf.

9th PA (2nd position)

2nd KY

9th OH

CONFEDERATE SKIRMISHERS

MCLAWS

Hardy

Fiser

Harrison

1st GA Regulars

32nd GA

(2nd position)

HARDEE

(SR 1781)

(SR 1780)

8

HARDEE'S ROUTE OF RETREAT

Elliott

Conner

"Smithville" (WARTIME COMMUNITY)

Magruder Road

Cape Fear River

Deep Ravine

Smith's 1865 Ferry

(NC 82)

TALIAFERRO

7

Elliott

(SR 1783)

4

1st SC

3

Lucas Battn.

1st SC Artillery

2nd SC

5

6

33rd IN

22nd WI

85th IN

19th MI

105th IL

79th OH

102nd IL

128th IL

Case

Rhett

Ravine

10:30 a.m.

WILLIAMS
XX CORPS

N
W   E
S

road, and Col. Daniel Dustin's Second Brigade on right, about four miles south of
Averasboro. By the time Ward arrived, Kilpatrick's cavalry and Hawley's Brigade of the 1st Division were already "hotly engaged" and in need of assistance,
their ammunition nearly exhausted. Ward directed Cogswell to advance his brigade to relieve Hawley, taking his place as the rest of the Federal units filed to
left and right, aligning on his position.[23]

Marching with Ward's leading division, Cogswell's Brigade arrived "prepared for battle" shortly after 9:00 a.m., deploying with three regiments in the

first line and three in the second. After
a few minutes in this position Ward's
order arrived to advance to the support
of his embattled comrades. Cogswell
acted swiftly, sending his skirmishers
forward followed by the main battle
line. Ward noted in his report of the action that his order was "at once rapidly
and quickly effected." To fill the space
assigned to him, however, Cogswell
had to realign his brigade with all six
regiments in the first line, leaving no
reserve to meet unanticipated contin-
gencies. While this was not a preferred
alignment and was in fact somewhat
dangerous, Cogswell could call upon
Hawley or one of the newly-arriving
brigades of Brig. Gen. Nathaniel J.
Jackson's division if any emergency
arose. Once redeployed, the brigade ad-

Brig. Gen.. Adin B. Underwood

Underwood, *Three Years of Service*

vanced about 250 yards to the vicinity of Smith's Farm. Cogswell's center was
now near the Smith house, where a lively skirmish developed.[24]

Cogswell's regiments were formed into a line of battle two ranks deep,
pushing a heavy screen of skirmishers forward—"almost as heavy as a line of
battle," Underwood recalled—to press the issue. Under the overall command of
Capt. Cyrus E. Graves of the 33rd Massachusetts, each regiment supplied about
two companies for the effort, their advance against "the South Carolina chivalry"
supported by the rest of the line.[25]

The initial Confederate position lay at roughly right angles to the roadway.
The Southerners were dug in behind modest earthworks, but the position was

strengthened by the marshes masking the approaches and "a battery, which enfiladed the line of direct approach." Slogging through the wet terrain, the Northern infantry immediately came under fire from concealed Confederate skirmishers. "A very hot skirmish" followed, recalled the 26th Wisconsin's Lt. Col. Winkler, which developed for about an hour. With the advance, reported Hartwell Osborn of the 55th Ohio, the enemy were "provoked to use artillery, having a battery placed to command the road." Some shells fell among the skirmishers, but many also carried to the main line of battle which made a more appealing target for the Southern gunners. To meet this threat, General Williams sent forward three Twentieth Corps artillery units—Batteries I and M of the 1st New York and C of the 1st Ohio—to silence the enemy guns.[26]

As the artillery went into battery, Cogswell's skirmishers edged their way forward against an enemy often unseen amid the swampy underbrush and thickening woods. Lead balls zipped through the damp air on missions of destruction, occasionally slashing through the flesh or shattering the bone of an unlucky victim. Under constant fire, with any semblance of lines impossible to maintain, the fight rapidly degenerated into innumerable contests of small groups and individuals, personal contests with death and mutilation the lot of the vanquished.

Hartwell Osborn

Underwood, *Three Years of Service*

Gradually, one tree or bush at a time, the Federals began to move perceptibly forward. Their left resting roughly along the Raleigh Road, skirmishers of the 55th Ohio eventually gained a footing in a pine forest to their front, while those of the 26th Wisconsin waded their way through underbrush and mire. Skirmishers from the other regiments struggled through knee-deep water to keep the pressure on the Confederate defenders. The going was very slow, but gradually Cogswell's soldiers pushed the Rebels back to a point near the far edge of the woods, where they could view the first line of Southern entrenchments. "From this point the line of the enemy was in plain view," Osborn explained, "and the effect of the shells from our guns was plainly visible." As he watched, shells fell among the defenders, causing havoc and casualties with each round.[27]

While Ward's division went into action, Nathaniel Jackson's First Division began arriving on the field, filing into line on Ward's right, followed by John W. Geary's Second Division. Although Williams wanted to launch a frontal assault against the Confederate position, he recognized the difficulties his men would face attacking across the broken and unstable ground. Instead, he determined to flank the Confederates out of the position by sending a brigade around their right to probe for a gap between the Southern flank and the Cape Fear River. This task fell to Case's brigade of Ward's Division, which gradually withdrew from the front line, formed into columns, and began moving to its left, around the Confederate right, feeling for the Rebel flank and seeking a location from which the desired assault could be launched on the enemy's flank and rear.[28]

While Case moved out, Cogswell sidestepped his battle line to fill as much as possible the gap created by Case's withdrawal. To help mask Case's move, Ward ordered Cogswell's and Dustin's brigades to increase their pressure on the Confederates to prevent them from reinforcing their right, where Case's assault would take place. Cogswell sent the order forward to Captain Graves who, moving about to direct the Federal advance under what Underwood termed "a galling fire," appeared heedless of the danger about him. By the time the flanking movement was ready to redeploy, the Confederate skirmishers had been completely driven in and the Rebel entrenchments unmasked in preparation for the impending assault. Further, fearing an attack on their center once the skirmishers were driven in, the Confederates dispatched reinforcements to the perceived threat—away from the flank against which Case was deploying for his attack.[29]

By 3:00 p.m. Hartwell Osborn could plainly see the colors of the Case's Brigade as it formed across the plain beyond the enemy's unsupported right. While Case's regiments were forming, Williams sent the First Division forward to form on Ward's right against the Confederate left, but the swampy nature of the ground prevented the Federals from accomplishing much in that sector. All this time, Cogswell's men faced the brunt of the enemy fire, pushing gamely forward while exchanging deadly greetings with often unseen adversaries. The unremitting pressure they brought to bear on the Confederates was exactly what Williams and Ward hoped for—a threat that would freeze the Rebels in place and prevent reinforcement of the threatened flank.[30]

By 4:00 p.m. the time had arrived. Williams gave the order for the whole line to move forward. Case's brigade sprang forward with a lusty cheer, his vigorous assault crushing the exposed Rebel right. At the same time, Cogswell and Dustin moved forward with both their skirmish and main lines. The sudden pressure was too much for Taliaferro's inexperienced South Carolinians, who fled their position, according to Osborn, "in such haste as to abandon guns, swords, and knapsacks, and many a souvenir was picked up by the pursuing force." Cogswell's men and the rest of the Union line advanced into and beyond the first line of works. While the battle line paused briefly for realignment, the skirmishers pushed forward after the retreating enemy.[31]

Taliaferro's men had held as long as possible and as Hardee planned, fell back and about 300 yards and rallied on the second line of battle. The Federals pursued, but Confederate resistance quickly stiffened. Cogswell sent additional skirmishers forward until fully 360 soldiers—the typical strength of a Federal field regiment at that time in the war—were deployed in his front against what Winkler considered a "stronger line of works" than their first position. After what Cogswell remembered as "several hours of good fighting for skirmishers, the enemy left another and stronger line of works and fell back a mile through and beyond a swamp to his main line of earth-works, the skirmishers pushing him all the while."[32]

The Northerners continued on, Cogswell's skirmishers fighting their way into and through yet another swamp, pressing the Rebels back 600 yards, as Underwood described it, "through dense woods, over ridges and down through swamps, wading through water knee deep to within a hundred and fifty paces of heavy works held in great force." The Southerners retired within their third and most substantial defensive works, leaving their dead and wounded in Union hands. As the Rebels retreated, Hardee sent General McLaw's Division forward to occupy the Confederate left, a good position from which to sweep the approaches to the primary Confederate line. As McLaws moved forward, the Federals paused to realign before launching a final assault.[33]

Emerging from the swamp, Alpheus Williams deployed Ward's Division, with Jackson on his right and two divisions of the Fourteenth Corps on his left, for a general assault on Hardee's position. Ward, in turn, deployed his division with Case's Brigade on the left, Cogswell's on the right, and Dustin's in reserve. With the redeployment complete, Cogswell sent his skirmishers ahead three times, but each time they were forced to fall back, reporting strong works heavily manned and covered by soft ground on the approaches. Cogswell reported this to Twentieth Corps headquarters, but Williams was determined to launch an assault. The preparations complete, the entire Federal line moved forward over "flat, swampy country thinly wooded" against what Osborn described as a "strong and well-defended position," sweeping the Confederate skirmishers before it until being met by "a storm of artillery and musketry fire" from the main enemy line. Through this hail of munitions Cogswell's regiments struggled, clearing the swamps before pausing to realigning their ranks under the cover of a hill one hundred and twenty-five yards from the Southern field works. "The nature of the ground precluded a rapid advance," Ward

Capt. Charles M. Stone

Underwood, *Three Years of Service*

wrote in his report, "it being very swampy and heavy. My line pressed steadily forward, driving the rebel line before it through the swamp and off a commanding ridge into works." The Federals continued on, crossing the swamp. ". . .The troops upon my left not coming up," recalled Ward, "and receiving a full flank fire, I was obliged to order a halt, my line being within 100 yards of the rebel works." There, a further advance being deemed too costly, the Union infantry continued to engage in what Winkler described as "sharp skirmishing" that "lasted until night."[34]

By the time the deadly firing drew to a close, rain began to fall over the countryside, drenching the living and dead alike. Cogswell's exhausted men threw up temporary earthworks; half of the brigade remained on watch while the other half attempted to get some rest as best they could on the cool, wet ground. Hardee realized his force was incapable of holding out any longer and retreated toward Smithfield that night. The losses at Averasboro are difficult to tabulate precisely. Southern sources on the subject are thin. Hardee left behind three pieces of artillery and about 500 casualties, including 178 dead and 175 captured, many of whom were also wounded. Official Federal losses totalled 682 men, 149 killed and missing and 533 wounded.[35] Cogswell's brigade, which had been engaged in the rambling fight all day, suffered the second highest brigade casualties after Hawley's. Among its officers, the brigade lost in killed or mortally wounded Lt. Wellington Barry of the 20th Connecticut, Capt. Charles M. Stone of the 55th Ohio, and Capt. Carl Schmidt and Lt. Francis R. Klein of the 26th Wisconsin.

* * *

Losses of Cogswell's Brigade at Averasboro[36]			
Regiment	Killed and Mortally Wounded	Wounded	Total*
20th CT	5	16	21
26th WI	7	11	18
33rd MA	1	11	12
55th OH	5	31	36
73rd OH	1	14	15
136th NY	3	15	18
TOTAL	21	99	120

* Does not include captured or missing men

The unopposed romp through South Carolina was over. War was still a serious, deadly affair. The day-long fight slowed Sherman's advance for only about twenty-four hours, causing Howard's wing to slow slightly so as not to outpace Slocum by too great a distance. In the end, Hardee's delaying action did not accomplish its intended purpose, as Sherman continued his march with little delay.[37] The Federal success was due in no small part to Cogswell's Brigade. Engaged from a little after 9:00 a.m. until dark, Cogswell's regiments were continually under fire in the center of the Union line, where they maintained almost continual contact and prevented the Confederates from shifting troops to threatened sectors. The result was that while Cogswell held Hardee's attention in the middle of the line, Case's brigade maneuvered for its decisive flanking assault. Receiving praise from many present on the field for his troops' steadfast conduct, Cogswell used his own report to commend the conduct of Capt. Graves for his "bravery, coolness and good judgment while commanding the skirmish line." The captain would later receive a brevet promotion to major in recognition of his services that day.

Following the action at Averasboro Johnston made a final and unsuccessful stand at Bentonville, where Nathaniel Hughes, historian of the Battle of Bentonville, concluded that "Cogswell's role [was] the most important of all" in restoring the Union lines and bringing about the victory. "Cogswell's timely and powerful attack," Hughes wrote, after "coming on the field with tired troops," restored the broken Union line and repulsed a determined Confederate attack. "It was a remarkable, if not decisive performance."[38]

With the defeat at Bentonville, Johnston retired toward Smithfield. On the 22nd, Sherman advanced toward Goldsboro, arriving there the same day. When all his forces were consolidated, the Northern general mustered about 80,000 troops. Johnston, collecting all his available forces around Smithfield, could muster little more than 18,000 effectives.[39] "We finished our campaign at ten this morning," Winkler wrote home on March 24. "It has been a long and toilsome one, but it is accomplished."[40] In this he was correct. Johnston agreed to a cease fire on April 13, followed soon thereafter by the surrender of his army.

The final result was made possible in no small part by the steadfast loyalty of the veteran troops commanded by Brig. Gen. William Cogswell, men who had seen the worst war had to offer, yet with peace so near did not shirk when duty called upon them to once again risk all for their cause. Because of their conduct, their next march would be a peaceful trek to the capital of the nation they helped preserve, where a place of honor awaited them in the ceremonial Grand Review.

Notes

1. Frederick H. Dyer, *A Compendium of the War of the Rebellion*, 3 vols. (New York, 1959), p. 456; Carl Schurz, letter to parents, April 24, 1864, Schurz Papers, Library of Congress.

2. Two excellent books have been written about the Battle of Bentonville. The first is Mark L. Bradley's *Last Stand in the Carolinas: The Battle of Bentonville* (Savas Publishing Co., 1995), and the second is Nathaniel Cheairs Hughes, Jr., *Bentonville: The Final Battle of Sherman & Johnston* (Chapel Hill, 1996). The quote in the main text is from the latter, 116; William K. Winkler, ed., *Letters of Frederick C. Winkler 1862 to 1865* (Milwaukee, 1963), 198.

3. "The Opposing Forces in the Campaign of the Carolinas," *The Way to Appomattox: Battles and Leaders of the Civil War* (New York, 1956), 697; Fox, 311.

4. James S. Pula, "The Sigel Regiment": A History of the 26th Wisconsin Volunteer Infantry, 1862-1865 (Savas Publishing Co., 1998); Fox, *Regimental Losses*, 311.

5. James S. Pula, "The Sigel Regiment" (unpublished manuscript), "Opposing Forces," 697.

6. U.S. War Department, *The War of the Rebellion: The Official Records of the Union and Confederate Armies,* 128 vols. (Washington, DC, 1890-1901), Series I, vol.

47, pt. 1, 821. Hereinafter cited as *OR*. All references are to Series I unless otherwise noted.

7. *Annual Report of the Adjutant General of the State of Wisconsin*, (Madison, 1866), 408; Frederick Buerstatte, letters, February 17, 18, 19, and 21, 1865, in the Library of Congress; *OR* 47, pt. 1, 143, 844; Winkler, *Letters*, 199.

8. *Annual Report*, 409; Buerstatte, February 22, 1865; *OR* 47 pt. 1, 783, 823.

9. *OR* 47, pt. 1, 823.

10. Winkler, *Letters*, 200; Mark Mayo Boatner, *The Civil War Dictionary* (New York, 1961), 126; *OR* 47, pt. 1, 143.

11. *OR* 47, pt. 1, 844, 845; Adin B. Underwood, *The Three Years' Service of the Thirty-Third Mass. Infantry Regiment 1862-1865* (Boston, 1881), 271.

12. Winkler, *Letters*, 202; *Annual Report*, 409.

13. Winkler, *Letters*, 20; Boatner, *Dictionary*, 126.

14. *Annual Report*, 409; Buerstatte, March 6 and 12, 1865; *OR* 47, pt. 1, 143, 823, 844; Underwood, 279.

15. Buerstatte, March 13 and 14, 1865; Winkler, *Letters*, 202; *OR* 47, pt. 1, 824.

16. *OR* 47, pt. 1, 143, 823-824; Hartwell Osborn, *Trials and Triumphs: The Record of the Fifty-Fifth Ohio Volunteer Infantry* (Chicago, 1904), 197-198.

17. Boatner, *Dictionary*, 126.

18. Ibid., 35; William DeLoss Love, *Wisconsin in the War of the Rebellion: A History of All Regiments and Batteries the State Has Sent to the Field, and Deeds of Her Citizens, Governors and Other Military Officers, and State and National Legislators to Suppress the Rebellion* (Chicago, 1866), 962; *Annual Report*, 409; *OR* 47, pt. 1, 824; Osborn, *Trials and Triumphs*, 198; Thomas Budd Van Horne, *History of the Army of the Cumberland; Its Organization, Campaigns, and Battles, Written at the Request of Major-General George H. Thomas Chiefly from His Private Military Journal and Official and Other Documents Furnished by Him* (Cincinnati, 1875), 313; Burke Davis, *Sherman's March* (New York, 1980), 225; Underwood, *Three Years' Service*, 280.

19. Davis, *Sherman's March*, 226.

20. *OR* 47, pt. 1, pt. 585, 783.

21. Boatner, *Dictionary*, 35; Love, *Wisconsin in the War*, 962; *Annual Report*, 409; *OR* 47, pt. 1, 824; Osborn, *Trials and Triumphs*, 198; Van Horne, *Army of the Cumberland*, 313.

22. Shelby Foote, *The Civil War: A Narrative, Red River to Appomattox* (New York, 1974), 827; Osborn, *Trials and Triumphs*, 199; Van Horne, *Army of the Cumberland*, 314; Underwood, *Three Years' Service*, 280.

23. Osborn, *Trials and Triumphs*, 198; Boatner, *Dictionary*, 35; Love, *Wisconsin in the War*, 962; *Annual Report*, 409; *OR* 47, pt. 1, 783, 824; Underwood, *Three Years' Service*, 281.

24. *OR* 47, pt. 1, 783, 824.

25. Underwood, *Three Years' Service*, 281; Van Horne, *Army of the Cumberland*, 314; Osborn, *Trials and Triumphs*, 198.

26. Van Horne, *Army of the Cumberland*, 314; William Augustus Croffut, *The Military and Civil History of Connecticut During the War of 1861-1865: Comprising a Detailed Account of the Various Regiments and Batteries, through March, Encampment, Bivouac, and Battle: Also Instances of Distinguished Personal Gallantry, and Biographical Sketches of Many Heroic Soldiers: Together With a Record of the Patriotic Action of Citizens at Home, and of the Liberal Support Furnished by the State in Its Executive and Legislative Departments* (New York, 1868), 769; Osborn, *Trials and Triumphs*, 198.

27. Osborn, *Trials and Triumphs*, 199.

28. *OR* 47, pt. 1, 586, 783.

29. Underwood, *Three Years' Service*, 281.

30. Osborn, *Trials and Triumphs*, 199; Van Horne, *Army of the Cumberland*, 314.

31. Ibid.; Foote, *The Civil War*, 827.

32. Winkler, *Letters*, 202-203; Osborn, *Trials and Triumphs*, 199; Love, *Wisconsin in the War*, 962; *Annual Report*, 409; *OR* 47, pt. 1, 824.

33. Underwood, *Three Years' Service*, 281; Foote, *The Civil War*, 827; Osborn, *Trials and Triumphs*, 199.

34. Osborn, *Trials and Triumphs*, 199; Van Horne, *Army of the Cumberland*, 314; Winkler, *Letters*, 202-203; Buerstatte, March 16, 1865; *OR* 47, pt. 1, 825.

35. Foote, *The Civil War*, 827-828; Winkler, *Letters*, 202-203; *OR* 47, pt. 1, 825; Van Horne, *Army of the Cumberland*, 314.

36. Losses compiled from various sources including Croffut, *Military and Civil History of Connecticut*, 770; Osborn, *Trials and Triumphs*, 200; William F. Fox, *Regimental Losses in the American Civil War, 1861-1865* (Albany, 1889), 328, 331, 399; *OR* 47, pt. 1, 64.

37. Boatner, *Dictionary*, 126; Winkler, *Letters*, 203; Love, *Wisconsin in the War*, 962; *Annual Report*, 409; *OR* 47, pt. 1, 844.

38. Hughes, *Bentonville*, 116, 188-119.

39. Boatner, *Dictionary*, 126-127.

40. Winkler, *Letters*, 203.

". . . pillage of every character, and destruction the most wanton."

"LIKE AN AVALANCHE"

George Stoneman's 1865 Cavalry Raid

Chris J. Hartley

I t began as ordinary rain, and later turned into a "furious hailstorm." Nevertheless, the weather that pounded the Knoxville, Tennessee area on Tuesday, March 21, 1865, did not deter the progress of war. That morning a long column of Union cavalrymen turned their mounts eastward and began one of the longest cavalry raids in history. Ahead lay western North Carolina and southwestern Virginia, a region of divided loyalties that had largely experienced the war only from a distance. This raid would change that. As a witness later stated, these Federal cavalrymen would roll over the area "like an avalanche," eliminating whatever slim hopes the Confederacy had for continuing the war.[1]

Six-foot-four Maj. Gen. George Stoneman, commander of the Union army's "District of East Tennessee," reviewed his men as they marched out of Knoxville. This force, the newly created Cavalry Division of the District of East Tennessee, contained about 5,000 men. Brigadier General Alvan C. Gillem held direct command of the division, which contained the brigades of Col. William J. Palmer, Brevet Brig. Gen. Simeon B. Brown, and Col. John K. Miller. Lieutenant James M. Regan led the four-gun battery that accompanied the raiders.[2]

Stoneman had been given command of the District of East Tennessee only the previous month, so he was eager to do a good job. Born August 22, 1822, in Busti, New York, Stoneman was an 1846 graduate of the United States Military Academy. A roommate there of Thomas J. Jackson, the New Yorker had subsequently enjoyed little of "Stonewall's" military success. During the Chancel-

Maj. Gen. George Stoneman

Library of Congress

lorsville Campaign, Stoneman had led the cavalry of the Army of the Potomac on a much criticized raid in the rear of Robert E. Lee's Army of Northern Virginia. In July 1864, while leading the Cavalry Corps of the Army of Ohio, he had been ingloriously captured while trying to destroy the Macon Railroad and liberate Union prisoners from Andersonville. Only recently had Stoneman's fortunes turned. In December 1864 he conducted a successful raid against the Tennessee and Virginia Railroad and the Saltville, Virginia salt works.[3]

Stoneman's objective for his latest raid was to hasten the end of the war. In the words of Ulysses S. Grant, commander-in-chief of all Union armies, Stoneman's expedition "goes to destroy and not to fight battles." Specifically, Maj. Gen. George H. Thomas, Stoneman's superior as commander of the Department of the Cumberland, instructed the New Yorker to head for southwest Virginia and western North Carolina and destroy parts of the East Tennessee and Virginia Railroad, the North Carolina Railroad, and the Piedmont Railroad. Their destruction hopefully would deny Robert E. Lee the use of those facilities in a possible retreat from Petersburg. Stoneman also received permission to raid the town of Salisbury, a major Confederate supply depot that also hosted a prisoner of war camp.[4]

Awaiting the raiders was a pitifully thin and scattered defense, placed in late March under the direction of Gen. P. G. T. Beauregard. The forty-six-year-old West Pointer had enjoyed success earlier in the war as second-in-command at Manassas and as commander of the South Carolina and Georgia coast defenses. Now, he faced one of the most difficult tasks of his career. "I could scarcely expect at this juncture," he wrote, "to be furnished with a force at all commensurate with the exigency or able to make head against the enemy reported advancing from East Tennessee towards Southwestern Virginia." Nonetheless, Beauregard and other Confederate officials did their best.[5]

Beauregard quickly saw that Salisbury, the key strategic point in the area, should be the focus of the Confederate defense. He ordered Lt. Gen. Stephen D. Lee, on his way to Raleigh with about 5,000 men to reinforce Joseph E. Johnston's Army of Tennessee, to pause in Salisbury. Confederate officials shuttled other units to the area as well, including the Mississippi horse soldiers of Samuel W. Ferguson. Beauregard also could not overlook the important communication centers of Greensboro and Danville, and so Joe Johnston sent artillery units to help guard those two towns. Beauregard also asked Johnston for cavalry support, but that was not immediately forthcoming. Meanwhile, North Carolina Governor Zebulon Vance ordered the state's ill-equipped, poorly trained home guards into action. General James G. Martin, the commander of the Confederate army's "District of Western North Carolina," readied his forces, but their distant position made their assistance unlikely. And in the "Department of Southwestern Virginia," Brig. Gen. John Echols counted about 4,000 infantrymen and 2,200 cavalrymen. None of this encouraged Beauregard. "I have not sufficient force to guard well at [the] same time this place [Greensboro], Salisbury, and Danville," he wrote.[6]

Meanwhile, on the morning of March 22, Stoneman's column continued its eastward march. Each man carried only five days' rations, a day's worth of forage, and four horseshoes and nails. All other supplies and fresh horses would be taken as needed. Over the next few days, the troopers moved quickly through east Tennessee. Ahead, rumors of the raid began to spread across the countryside, and its citizens prepared for the worse. In the Moravian church community of Salem, for example, the students of the local college hid money and jewelry under a stone in the cellar of the principal's house. Elsewhere, in the mountain town of Pleasant Gardens, a young teacher helped hide away hams, money, and clothes in "the biggest burying I ever attended."[7]

On March 28, the raiders entered North Carolina. As they rode toward Boone, troopers learned that a meeting of the local home guard was scheduled for that very day. Stoneman sent his young aide-de-camp, Capt. Miles Keogh, and a detachment from the 12th Kentucky Cavalry to disperse the home guard. Keogh was a born fighter, an Irish-born soldier of fortune who already had served with the French Foreign Legion in Africa and with the Papal Guard in Italy. In 1876, he would be among the last to fall at the Battle of Little Bighorn. On this day, Keogh's Federals rode irresistibly into Boone, firing at anything that moved.[8]

Home guardsmen, citizens, and Confederate soldiers on leave tried to fight back. Calvin Green initially surrendered, but when Federals continued firing in his direction, he grabbed a weapon and responded in kind. One of his shots shattered the arm of a Federal trooper. Fifteen-year-old Steele Frazier, chased by a half-dozen Federals, ducked behind a fence and gunned down a pursuer. He retreated, killed another, and then escaped. Several men from the Confederate 1st North Carolina Cavalry Regiment also were in Boone and doubtless resisted, but the end was predictable. As a trooper from the 10th Michigan Cavalry recorded: "They ran so like the old cat we could not hardly get a sight of them but thanks that my good horse can run like a streak of lightening and I made out to get about a dozen shots at them and I think I emptied one of their saddles." When the smoke cleared, the Federals had killed nine and captured 68, plundered a few homes, and burned the local jail and its records.[9]

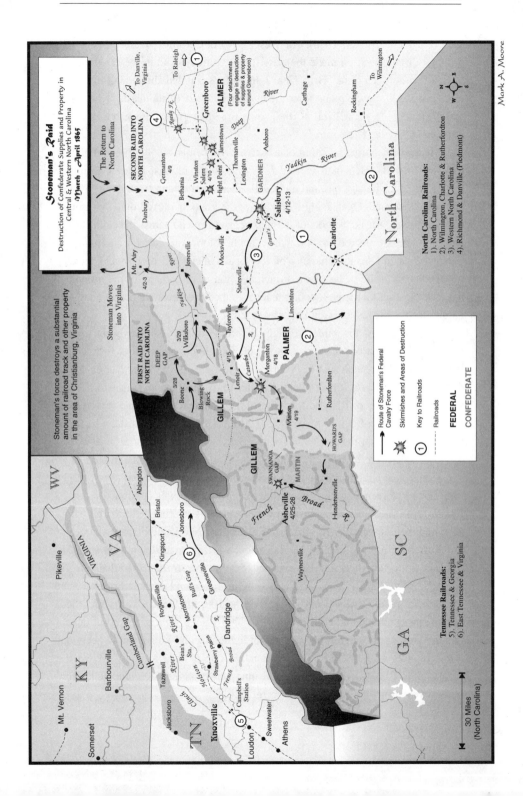

Mark A. Moore

Stoneman's Raid

Destruction of Confederate Supplies and Property in
Central & Western North Carolina
March – April 1865

The Return to
North Carolina

Stoneman's force destroys a substantial
amount of railroad track and other property
in the area of Christianburg, Virginia.

Stoneman Moves
into Virginia

**SECOND RAID INTO
NORTH CAROLINA**

Germanton
4/9

Winston
Salem 4/10
High Point

GARDNER

Salisbury
4/12-13

(Four detachments
engage in destruction
of supplies & property
around Greensboro)

PALMER

Greenboro

To Danville,
Virginia

To Raleigh

To Wilmington

Danbury

Bethania

Mt. Airy
4/2-3

Jonesville

Mocksville

Statesville

**FIRST RAID INTO
NORTH CAROLINA**

DEEP
GAP

3/28

Boone

Blowing
Rock

GILLEM

Wilkesboro
3/29

Taylorsville

4/15

Lenoir

Morganton
4/18

PALMER

Lincolnton

Charlotte

Jamestown

Thomasville
Lexington

Ashboro

Reedy Fk.

Deep River

Yadkin River

Carthage

Rockingham

To Wilmington

North Carolina

Grant's Cr.

Catawba R.

Yadkin River

Marion
4/19

HOWARD'S
GAP

Rutherfordton

GILLEM

SWANNANOA
GAP

MARTIN

Asheville
4/25-26

Hendersonville

French Broad R.

Broad R.

Waynesville

GA

SC

Route of Stoneman's Federal
Cavalry Force

Skirmishes and Areas of Destruction

Key to Railroads

Railroads

FEDERAL

CONFEDERATE

WV

VIRGINIA

VA

Pikeville

Mt. Vernon

Somerset

KY

Barbourville

Jacksboro

Tazewell

Cumberland Gap

Abingdon

Bristol

Kingsport

Rogersville

Jonesboro

Morristown

Bull's Gap

Greeneville

Dandridge

Bean's
Sta.

Strawberry Plains

Campbell's
Station

Knoxville

Loudon

Sweetwater

Athens

TN

Clinch River

Holston River

French Broad R.

Little R.

Tennessee Railroads:
5). Tennessee & Georgia
6). East Tennessee & Virginia

North Carolina Railroads:
1). North Carolina
2). Wilmington, Charlotte & Rutherfordton
3). Western North Carolina
4). Richmond & Danville (Piedmont)

30 Miles
(North Carolina)

N
W   E
S

Following the Boone skirmish, Stoneman decided to leave the Blue Ridge Mountains and move to Wilkesboro to obtain supplies and fresh horses. He separated his command to accomplish this. Gillem took Brown's brigade of Kentucky and Michigan men, Miller's brigade of Tennessee troopers, and the artillery, moving by way of Patterson's factory near Lenoir. Gillem, born in Gainesboro, Tennessee on July 29, 1830, was an 1851 graduate of West Point. He had spent much of the war serving in the difficult position of Adjutant General of Tennessee. He also had commanded the forces that killed the famous Confederate raider, John Hunt Morgan. In contrast to his earlier experiences, his movement on Patterson's Factory seemed simple. At 9:00 p.m., Gillem reached the cotton mill and surprised the workers. After sampling the corn and bacon stored there, the column spent the night and then moved on to Wilkesboro, leaving behind a rear guard to destroy the factory and any remaining supplies. According to a witness, the finely equipped and disciplined Federals were not allowed to plunder or commit any acts of violence during their stay at Patterson's.[10]

Stoneman, meanwhile, with Palmer's brigade of Pennsylvania, Michigan, and Ohio men, took the direct route to Wilkesboro through Deep Gap. Late in the afternoon of March 29, Gillem and Stoneman reunited just outside Wilkesboro. As dark rain clouds gathered overhead, Stoneman sent the 12th Ohio Cavalry into Wilkesboro. Local merchant Calvin J. Cowles watched as "they came in with a yell and ran completely through the place, frightening a small body of Confederates out of their wits and out of the place."[11]

Stoneman did not care to dawdle in the Wilkesboro area, but the weather failed to cooperate. Just as his troopers began crossing the Yadkin River to head north, "the very heavens . . . opened their floodgates," one trooper remembered. Quickly the river rose until it became impassable, separating the Federal command. At least one man drowned during the aborted crossing. While the Federals waited for the rain to stop, they raided the countryside and found a few moonshine stills. The water fell in sheets and the mud was knee-deep, but that did not prevent the soldiers from getting drunk and riding around town in captured wagons, coaches, and carriages. An angry Stoneman railed at the men and his staff, and even ordered a review, but he could not stop the party.[12]

Three days passed before Stoneman was finally able to ford the Yadkin River and get his men moving. The Federals did not simply wait for the waters to recede, however. They torched key factories in the area, burning 800 bales of cotton at one location. On April 2, the Federals pointed their horses north toward Virginia. This change of direction ultimately altered the Confederate defensive stance. When reports of this movement found their way to Beauregard, he figured the threat to Salisbury had ended. The Confederate general began shifting troops from there to Greensboro and Danville. He even canceled his request for the cavalry forces of Gen. Joseph Wheeler from Johnston's army, and asked only that a single cavalry regiment be dispatched to Danville.[13]

Stoneman's route to the Virginia border led through Surry County. Like every day of the raid, this was an eventful one for the locals. At one point, a few blue-coated cavalrymen stopped at a farm, bound its owner, and ordered his wife to cook dinner. She replied that she could not unless they untied her husband so he could fetch water. The men got their dinner. Elsewhere, near Siloam, a recuperating Confederate and a local citizen clashed with a contingent of Federal cavalry. Other raiders met up with E. T. Clemmons, who was on a trip from Forsyth County to Wytheville. They relieved Clemmons and his servant of their horses, exchanging them for broken down mounts. And the next day, near Hillsville, Virginia, the Federals captured 17 Confederate wagons filled with forage.[14]

Although Stoneman encountered more resistance in Virginia, the raid continued unabated. At Hillsville, the Federal general divided his force so he could destroy as much of the Virginia and Tennessee Railroad as possible. He ordered Colonel Miller to take 500 men from his brigade to Wytheville and break apart the railroad bridges there. Miller, a clean-shaven, staunch Unionist from Carter County, Tennessee, ran into trouble at Wytheville when Confederates under Gen. John C. Vaughn and Col. Henry Giltner attacked his column. Miller's men managed to accomplish their mission but ultimately withdrew after suffering 35 casualties. "We had been fighting a largely superior force of the enemy and had he had the fighting qualities of other days our chances of escape would have been slim," recalled one Federal cavalryman. Afterward, Miller retired to Hillsville and then to Taylorsville, Virginia.[15]

As Miller clashed with the enemy and burned bridges, Stoneman took the rest of the division toward Jacksonville. A few Confederates provided slight resistance that evening, but the Federals brushed them aside. On April 4, while Lee's Army of Northern Virginia was retreating westward from the trenches of Richmond and Petersburg, two citizens bearing a white flag met the Unionists and tried to surrender the town. "It looked to us ridiculous," wrote one Pennsylvania trooper, "as just now anything we wanted we took. But these people have been so deluded by their papers that they are under the impression that to burn houses and rob them of all we can carry off is our mission here, and they are relieved when they find the mistake." From Jacksonville, the bulk of Stoneman's command moved on Christianburg, tearing up railroad tracks east and west of town on April 5. Stoneman had now destroyed more than 150 miles of the Virginia and Tennessee Railroad. As a final gesture, he also sent another detachment, this one from the 15th Pennsylvania Cavalry, to create havoc as far as the outskirts of Lynchburg. After the war, veterans of this detachment would claim that their Lynchburg raid played a role in the surrender of the Army of Northern Virginia at nearby Appomattox Court House.[16]

Stoneman set his forces in motion to return to North Carolina on April 7. Brown's and Miller's brigades moved south through Patrick County toward the state line. As they had all along the route, the Federals continued to forage for supplies and fresh mounts. At the home of Thomas Shelton, Federal troopers took one sorrel mare, 300 pounds of bacon, 25 bushels of corn, 500 pounds of fodder, 25 fowls, a rifle, and two silver watches. Palmer's brigade, though, had a rougher time of it. They rode south by mistake through neighboring Henry County. At 7:00 a.m. on April 8, about 250 Confederate cavalrymen under Col. J. T. Wheeler met Palmer in the streets of Martinsville. The encounter left one Union trooper dead and five others wounded. In return, the Federals captured about 20 horses and repulsed the Confederates. Wheeler, who reported his losses as minimal, estimated the enemy at 800 strong. He withdrew his regiment toward Danville but kept a wary eye on the Federal horse soldiers.[17]

On April 9—the day of General Lee's surrender at Appomattox Court House—the bulk of Stoneman's command reunited in North Carolina. Stoneman turned his attention to his next objectives: the clothing factories and rail lines around Salem and Greensboro, and the town of Salisbury itself. He detached Palmer's brigade to Salem and then continued southward with the rest of the division. At daylight on April 11, Stoneman reached Shallow Ford, an old crossing of the Yadkin River that had been the scene of a Revolutionary War skirmish. There, his forces captured 100 muskets after chasing off a small enemy detachment. Shallow Ford would be Stoneman's springboard for the attack on Salisbury.[18]

With the ford secured, the command turned to foraging. Mrs. Sarah Dalton, an elderly woman who lived nearby, heard a knock on her door at about 7:00 a.m. An officer of John Miller's command stood on her doorstep. He "asked in a very respectful manner," Mrs. Dalton later stated, "for breakfast for fifteen (15) officers." She agreed and went to work. To her chagrin, hungry guests continued to arrive, and the Federal officer added that their cavalry stock would feed from her corn crib as well. By 4:00 that afternoon, Mrs. Dalton had fed about 100 Union soldiers and her corn crib had supplied three or four thousand horses.[19]

While Stoneman's men and horses feasted, Palmer's brigade advanced on the neighboring towns of Winston and Salem. John W. Fries, a Salem business-man, was on scout duty that day with about six other volunteers. "I saw the heads of two men as they came to the top of the hill ahead of us," Fries remembered, "and by the time we could turn and start back, they were coming in a gallop, and shooting as they came. I do not know how often they shot, but I distinctly heard the whistle of two bullets." The Federals captured one of the scouts, but Fries escaped. He spread word of the Federal advance.[20]

Despite Fries's warning, Palmer carried out his assignment to Stoneman's "entire satisfaction." The colonel accepted the surrender of Winston and Salem from their respective leaders. The towns escaped harm; the local newspaper reported that the Federals strictly respected private persons and property. A few locals even provoked their guests, but the Federals only laughed at their chal-lenges. On one occasion, a young Salem Female Academy student from Ala-bama waved a Confederate flag and let loose with a "Rebel Yell." In a display of feeble-mindedness, the town clerk's son boasted to some passing cavalrymen, "You can't get our horses; we got 'em hid in the cellar."[21]

Palmer next sent men out into the countryside east of Salem to search for bridges, factories, and railroad facilities. One detachment captured and burned the Dan River Bridge, cutting a vital link in the Piedmont Railroad. (Confeder-ate President Jefferson Davis had just traveled over that same bridge as he fled to Greensboro with what remained of his government and treasury.) Another detachment routed the 3rd South Carolina Cavalry near Greensboro and then burned the Buffalo Creek Bridge. At High Point, a North Carolina Railroad depot, yet another group of raiders destroyed property estimated at $4 million. However, elements of Palmer's brigade also ran into stiff resistance in the area. General Samuel W. Ferguson's cavalry brigade, for example, "furiously at-tacked" the raiders near Lexington and Thomasville, south of Salem. According to a trooper from the 10th Michigan Cavalry, "this was the most trying attack in which the regiment has been engaged and nothing but the cool bearing of officers and men averted a serious disaster." Finally, on April 11, Palmer with-drew his brigade to Shallow Ford. His men would rejoin the cavalry division late the next day.[22] They found the division at Salisbury, because Stoneman had already left Shallow Ford to assault the town. The horse soldiers were eager to liberate their comrades from the prisoner of war camp located there. Unfortu-nately for the raiders, the prison had recently been evacuated to a more secure location. The raiding cavalrymen would have to be satisfied with capturing

Salisbury itself. By 8:00 p.m. on April 11, Stoneman bivouacked his troops in the rainy darkness just 12 miles north of town.[23]

The Federals moved out shortly after midnight. Within a short time they reached the South Yadkin, a "deep and rapid stream with but few fords." Crossing the river unopposed, the Federal troopers marched until they reached a fork in the road. Since both roads led to Salisbury, Stoneman sent one battalion of the 12th Kentucky Cavalry by the old road. He instructed the Kentuckians to demonstrate at Grant's Creek, which formed a natural defensive barrier two miles outside of town. If they could cross, they were to take the Confederates defending the upper road's bridge from the rear. Meanwhile, the main body took the western road.[24]

Daylight of April 12 brought the heaviest fighting of the raid. The main column neared Grant's Creek and chased away some pickets. Across the creek waited a hodgepodge force of less than 500 Confederates and two batteries of artillery. The defenders included 200 "galvanized" Irishmen who had been recruited from Federal prisoners, several Junior Reserves, some local citizens, and even a few Confederate government employees. As the Federals reached the bridge, the defenders opened fire; in the distance echoed the sound of trains hurrying from the threatened town.[25]

Since Beauregard had also called the current commander of Salisbury, Brig. Gen. Bradley T. Johnson, to Greensboro, Brig. Gen. William M. Gardner was now in command. Gardner, a West Pointer, had spent most of the war in administrative tasks after suffering a crippling leg wound at First Manassas. Most recently he had been commandant of the military garrison at Richmond, and had only just arrived in Salisbury after the evacuation of the capital city. John C. Pemberton, the defeated former commander of Confederate forces at Vicksburg, also had recently arrived. Pemberton had resigned his general's commission in 1864, but later accepted a commission as lieutenant colonel of artillery in the Richmond defenses. With Pemberton probably assisting the artillery, Gardner directed the defenses of his adopted force along Grant's Creek. The general ordered the flooring of the bridge removed to hinder a Federal crossing.[26]

Rather than risk a direct assault, Stoneman ordered Gillem to send out additional flanking elements. Gillem assigned 100 men from the 13th Tennessee Cavalry to cross Grant's Creek below the enemy position while another detachment crossed the creek even farther down stream. Gillem also ordered a detachment of the 11th Kentucky Cavalry to cross the creek two and a half miles above the bridge and strike for the railroad and the rear of the town. Keogh accompanied the Kentuckians.[27]

Gillem waited with the main body until the rattling fire of Spencer rifles confirmed that the enemy's flanks had been turned. Miller's Tennessee brigade was ordered to advance. The Tennesseans dismounted and prepared to push forward. As one Federal got off his very conspicuous white horse, a shell burst overhead, scaring the horse and causing him to throw his rider. Other than that single incident, however, Miller's men had little trouble. They paused only to repair the bridge, and then charged across the creek. Brown's brigade moved up in support, and the Confederates began falling back toward town.[28]

The running engagement swirled into Salisbury. One young girl watched as the road in front of her house became "jammed with a surging mass of mounted soldiers and rampant horses spurred to a breakneck speed. . . ." Twenty-four-year-old Margaret Ellen Beall also saw the Unionists, and she never forgot the moment when the fighting reached her home. "The missiles were flying thick and fast around and upon the house," she wrote. "Then plunging their horses over the fence, some of the soldiers rushed into the hall and up the steps, demanding of me, 'the damned rebel who lives here.' Downstairs the men were ransacking, pillaging, wielding their swords among the terrified servants and shouting, 'Make me some coffee! Fry me some meat! Make me some bread or I'll cut you in two!'" Outside, a Confederate lieutenant from Maryland waged his own battle. Chased by a Federal officer, the Confederate suddenly reigned in his horse, let the Northerner pass, and then shot him to death. Even Miles Keogh came under fire and received a severe wound in the left knee.[29]

The Federals soon had Salisbury in hand, along with its rich haul. Stoneman counted 17 stands of colors, 18 artillery pieces and about 1,300 prisoners for his efforts. The raiders also destroyed 10,000 stands of small arms, 10,000 artillery rounds, 1 million rounds of small arms ammunition, 70,000 pounds of powder, 160,000 pounds of bacon, 100,000 uniforms, 20,000 pounds of harness leather, 10,000 pounds of saltpeter, 35,000 bushels of corn, 50,000 bushels of wheat, sugar, salt, rice and other stores, and medical supplies valued at $100,000. Four cotton factories were captured, as well as the hated—but empty—prison. Fifteen miles of track along with the depot of the North Carolina Railroad and the car shops of the Western North Carolina line were burned. The Federals even seized a passenger train on the WNC tracks, finding on board the possessions and family of the late Confederate general, Leonidas Polk.[30]

One more prize remained to be taken. The important railroad bridge over the Yadkin River, six miles above town, was still standing, so Stoneman sent a detachment to capture the structure. The bridge site was the scene of Beauregard's single defensive success of the entire raid, as well as one of the war's final

Confederate victories. Beauregard had dispatched about 1,000 men, including home guards and galvanized Confederates, to hold the bridge at all hazards. General Zebulon York, a native of Maine and a veteran of the Army of Northern Virginia, commanded the defenders. Fighting erupted as the Union detachment approached the structure. The Confederates, entrenched on the high bluffs across the river, poured down a heavy fire. The stalled Union troops brought up recently-captured artillery from Salisbury to shell the Secessionists, but the effort proved unsuccessful. At nightfall on April 12, the Federals returned to Salisbury without attempting a crossing. A handful of Confederates had been wounded and one or two killed in the fight.[31]

Stoneman did not mark time at Salisbury. While Palmer's brigade moved toward Charlotte to destroy more railroad track and the 1,125-foot railroad bridge over the Catawba River, the rest of the cavalry division left Salisbury at 3:00 p.m. on April 13. Their destination was Statesville, a depot of the Western North Carolina Railroad. Reaching it without trouble, the advance guard entered Statesville firing as they went. They detained a few citizens and shot and wounded another when he ran from his home. The Federals occupied Statesville only for a few hours, long enough to destroy some government stores, the railroad depot, and the office of the *Iredell Express* newspaper. According to 19 year-old diarist Annie Olympia Donnell, a dozen "old dirty and worn out socks" were among the items the Federals left behind.[32]

Stoneman headed west, but hours later Palmer's men arrived in Statesville from their raid toward Charlotte and the South Carolina border. The brigade remained there until April 17, skirmishing with various Confederate cavalry detachments, including men from Samuel W. Ferguson's command. Stoneman ordered Palmer to establish headquarters at Lincolnton and "watch the line of the Catawba" River. From there, the Federals could either continue operations against Charlotte or harass the flank of any army moving south.[33]

Their ride to Lincolnton would not be uneventful, thanks to the recent arrival of other Southern horse soldiers to the area. These were the Confederate cavalrymen of John Echols' Southwestern Virginia command, who reached Statesville after Palmer left. The previous week, Echols had ordered his cavalrymen into North Carolina to join General Johnston after he learned of Lee's surrender. Accordingly, the brigades of Basil W. Duke and John Vaughn, plus a portion of Giltner's Brigade, entered the state by way of Fancy Gap. As they crossed the Yadkin near Yadkinville and rode toward Statesville, Duke's men cut a particularly unseemly profile: they rode on mules since their horses had been sent to Lincolnton during the winter to forage.[34]

From Statesville, Echols rode alone to Salisbury to search for General Johnston. He instructed Vaughn to move toward Morganton, and sent Duke's Brigade toward Lincolnton to find their horses. It was then that Duke discovered Palmer's Federal cavalrymen also marching on a parallel road to the same destination. The two forces began skirmishing on side roads that connected their routes. To Duke's chagrin, his foe got the better of his men. "When I inquired the reason," he recalled, "every fellow said it was the fault of his 'infernal mule,' which could not possibly be induced to behave reasonably in action." Ultimately, the Federals reached Lincolnton first, forcing Duke to bypass the town. He did manage to link up with his horse detail, which luckily had escaped Palmer's grasp. Duke's and Vaughn's men continued on to Charlotte, where they joined Ferguson's Brigade and a few other units and became part of President Davis's escort.[35]

West of Lincolnton, Miller's and Brown's Federal brigades passed through Taylorsville and reached Lenoir on Easter Sunday. Gillem thought Lenoir "a rebellious little hole," but Stoneman's presence prevented the troops from excessive mischief. The troopers paused to shake down their prisoners and refit the artillery. Stoneman, who by then had heard rumors of Lee's surrender, decided that he had completed his mission. On April 17, he left the division for East Tennessee, taking with him more than 1,000 prisoners. He directed Gillem to continue the raid and move the second and third brigades toward Asheville.[36]

Gillem did so, but marched only a short distance before he found Confederates guarding a bridge over the Catawba River, near Rocky Ford just east of Morganton. Brigadier General John P. McCown directed the contingent. At Murfreesboro, McCown had commanded a division of the Army of Tennessee; on this day his company-sized command numbered about 80 men, mostly home guards and local citizens. The defenders had prepared breastworks and rifle pits along the river banks, and positioned their lone artillery piece nearby. Other men formed in support along a wooded hill near the river bank.[37]

As the two Union brigades approached, the Confederate artillery piece opened fire and momentarily stymied the Federals. Gillem reacted quickly. More than once he sent his men headlong toward the position, but the defenders somehow held. Gillem dispatched a battalion of the 8th Tennessee Cavalry to flank the position while he readied another battalion to cross the bridge. Regan's Federal battery opened fire, and within a short time the single Confederate gun was dismounted. The Tennesseeans charged the position and broke through the thin line of defenders. "The Home Guards and the other troops did their duty," a witness recalled, "but were greatly outnumbered." The Southerners lost only two wounded in the affair, but claimed they inflicted as many as 28 casualties, including 11 killed.[38]

Morganton fell in due course. "The streets were full of blue coats," remembered one citizen, "and the air resounded with the shouts, yells, & terrible oaths" of the Federal soldiers. The troopers quickly turned to foraging, and by nightfall they had visited nearly every house in the village. The plight of Mrs. Margaret Williams was typical. The poor woman "contributed" 50 pounds of bacon, a mule, a sorrel mare, a saddle, and a bridle to the raiders. She later appealed to both Gillem and Brown, to no avail. These officers were more interested in their next objective: Asheville.[39]

Like Morganton, the mountain town of Asheville would not go undefended. General James G. Martin, the commander of the "District of Western North Carolina," had expected the Federals to come calling. Called "Old One Wing" because he had lost an arm in the Mexican War, Martin moved his command—John B. Palmer's Brigade of North Carolinians and James R. Love's regiment of William H. Thomas's Legion—to the Swannanoa Gap area to defend the direct approach to Asheville. Trees were felled and defenses prepareds to receive the enemy.[40]

The Union raiders reached Swannanoa Gap on April 20 and found it stoutly blocked by about 500 men and four pieces of artillery. The Confederates had done a good job of obstructing the pass. One Federal thought "it would take a month to clean out that road." Gillem again resorted to his favorite maneuver. He ordered Miller to remain at the gap and "deceive the enemy by feints" while he made a forced march with Brown's brigade to outflank the Confederate right. The mountainous terrain forced the horse soldiers to make a wide flanking movement. On April 21 Gillem reached Rutherfordton, more than 20 miles southeast of Swannanoa Gap. By dusk the next day the Federals had brushed aside "slight resistance" and crossed the Blue Ridge at Howard's Gap. Gillem now lay squarely astride Martin's flank.[41]

The ruse did not deceive General Martin, who was a veteran of the terrible fighting at Petersburg. He sent troops to meet the Federals at the mountain crossings below Swannanoa Gap. On April 22, however, rumors filtered westward that Joseph E. Johnston had surrendered to William T. Sherman near Durham. On the basis of this news, Martin's men wisely refused to obey his order to stand and fight. That evening, Gillem negotiated the surrender of the gap with little problem.[42]

With a Blue Ridge pass now in Federal hands, Gillem continued his march on Asheville. He also summoned Palmer's brigade, still at Lincolnton, to Rutherfordton in support. On Sunday afternoon, April 23, the Confederates again halted the Union advance, only this time with a flag of truce. Having received official notification of Johnston's and Lee's surrenders, Martin arranged to meet Gillem the next morning to discuss surrender terms. Later that day, Gillem received official confirmation from Sherman that both Lee and Johnston had indeed capitulated.[43]

The meeting between Martin and Gillem "went off quietly and in order," Martin later wrote. The Confederates agreed to cease resistance, following the terms Sherman had granted to Johnston. Gillem accepted, and on April 25 the Federals began withdrawing to their Tennessee base. Gillem rode ahead to join the Tennessee legislature, which was then assembling, leaving Palmer in command. The next day, however, Federal troopers returned to Asheville and sacked it. According to one horse soldier, the men had returned to the town on new orders and attacked when the Confederates refused to let them pass. At any rate, the locals never forgot the result. "Asheville will never again hear such sounds and witness such scenes—pillage of every character, and destruction the most wanton," recalled a citizen.[44]

One last duty remained for Stoneman's raiders, and it took nearly three weeks to accomplish it. Jefferson Davis and the remains of the Confederate government continued to flee—and the cavalry division was in position to pursue. On April 23, Palmer learned of Lincoln's assassination and received orders to chase Jefferson Davis to "the ends of the earth." Accordingly, Palmer pushed his force into South Carolina and then Georgia. They narrowly missed capturing the fugitive president on several occasions, but as a consolation the division did capture generals Braxton Bragg and Joseph Wheeler. Finally, on May 15, another Federal unit captured Davis near Irwin, Georgia. But as General Thomas remarked to his staff, the Cavalry Division of the District of East Tennessee still could be proud. "General [James] Wilson held the bag," Thomas said, "and Palmer drove the game into it."[45]

There were more reasons for boasting. While the events of Appomattox Court House and Bennett Place understandably overshadowed George Stoneman's 1865 Raid in North Carolina and Virginia, its exploits were memorable. Traveling more than one thousand miles through enemy territory, the Cavalry Division of East Tennessee took the last breath of the rebellion. The Federals captured 46 artillery pieces, 6,000 prisoners, and 17 battle-flags. They demolished uncountable tons of supplies. Most importantly, they destroyed vital railroad track, bridges, rolling stock, and depots. In the words of General Sherman, the "sad havoc" they wreaked was fatal to the armies of the Confederacy.

Stoneman's raiders eliminated the supplies, reinforcements, and line of retreat that Joe Johnston and Robert E. Lee would have required to continue the struggle. Without such an infrastructure, the rebellion died.[46]

(The author would like to thank Wayne Boone, F. Brad Bush, Sue Curtis, Robert E. L. Krick, Joe Linn, and Horace Mewborn for their assistance.)

Notes

1. Charles H. Kirk, ed., *History of the Fifteenth Pennsylvania Volunteer Cavalry* (Philadelphia, 1906), 524, 492-493; Calvin J. Cowles to ?, June 22, 1866, Calvin J. Cowles Papers, North Carolina State Archives, Raleigh, NC (hereinafter cited as NCSA).

2. U.S. War Department, *The War of the Rebellion: The Official Records of the Union and Confederate Armies*, 128 vols. (Washington, DC, 1890-1901), Series I, vol. 49, pt. 1, 325-326. Hereinafter cited as *OR*. All references are to series I unless otherwise stated; *OR* 36, pt. 1, 50. Suzanne Colton Wilson, comp., *Column South with the Fifteenth Pennsylvania Cavalry* (Flagstaff, AZ, 1960), 276; Kirk, *Fifteenth Pennsylvania Cavalry*, 520. Palmer's brigade included the 10th Michigan, 12th Ohio, and 15th Pennsylvania Cavalry; Brown's the 11th and 12th Kentucky and the 11th Michigan; and Miller's brigade included the 8th, 9th, and 13th Tennessee Cavalry.

3. Ezra J. Warner, *Generals In Blue: Lives of the Union Commanders* (Baton Rouge, 1964), 481-482; James I. Robertson, Jr., *Stonewall Jackson: The Man, The Soldier, The Legend* (New York, 1997), 40; Ina W. Van Noppen, *Stoneman's Last Raid* (Raleigh, NC, 1961), 3-4.

4. *OR* 49, pt. 1, 616; pt. 2, 17; *OR* 47, pt. 3, 777; Van Noppen, *Stoneman's Raid*, pp. 7-8; John G. Barrett, *The Civil War in North Carolina* (Chapel Hill, NC, 1963), 350.

5. Ezra J. Warner, *Generals in Gray: Lives of the Confederate Commanders* (Baton Rouge, 1959), 22-23; Alfred Roman, *The Military Operations of General Beauregard*, 2 vols. (1884; reprint, New York, 1994), vol. 1, 383; *OR* 47, pt. 3, 719, 723ff.

6. Van Noppen, *Stoneman's Raid*, 12; *OR* 47, pt. 3, 722-727; *OR* 49, pt. 1, 1044; Basil W. Duke, "Last Days of the Confederacy," in Robert U. Johnson and Clarence C. Buell, eds., *Battles & Leaders of the Civil War*, 4 vols. (1884-89; reprint, New York, n.d.), vol. 4, 762; R. L. Downs, "About the Time of the 'Surrender,'" photocopy of a series published in the *Lenoir Topic*, December 17, 1890-January 14, 1891.

7. *OR* 49, pt. 1, 330; Douglas LeTell Rights, "Salem in the War Between the States," *The North Carolina Historical Review*, July 1950, 286; Adelaide H. Fries et. al., *Forsyth: the History of A County on the March* (Chapel Hill, 1976), 141; Kirk, *Fifteenth Pennsylvania Cavalry*, p. 500; Emma L. Rankin, "Stoneman's Raid," in *In Memoriam, E. L. R.*,

24, Emma L. Rankin Papers, #621-z, Southern Historical Collection, University of North Carolina at Chapel Hill (hereinafter cited as SHC).

8. *OR* 49, pt. 1, 330-331; Cornelia Phillips Spencer, *The Last Ninety Days of the War in North-Carolina* (New York, 1866), p. 193; Evan S. Connell, *Son of the Morning Star: Custer and The Little Bighorn* (San Francisco, 1984), 290-294. Keogh's horse, Comanche, is said to have been the only survivor of Custer's Last Stand.

9. Robert E. Jones, *The Last Raid*, n.d., n.p., photocopy in possession of the author; Spencer, *Last Ninety Days*, 193-194; Chris J. Hartley, *Roster of the 1st North Carolina Cavalry*, n.p.; *OR* 49, pt. 1, 330-331; Spencer, *Last Ninety Days*, 193.

10. *OR* 49, pt. 1, 323, 331; Warner, *Generals in Blue*, 175-76; J. C. Norwood to Walter W. Lenoir, April 2, 1865, in Thomas F. Hickerson, *Echoes of Happy Valley* (Chapel Hill, NC, 1962), 104.

11. *OR* 49, pt. 1, 331; Calvin J. Cowles to Reverend C.R. Reddick, March 29, 1865 and Calvin J. Cowles to Arthur Cowles, April 6, 1865, Calvin J. Cowles Papers, NCSA.

12. Kirk, *Fifteenth Pennsylvania Cavalry*, 522-524.

13. R.L. Beall to Cornelia Phillips Spencer, n.d., 2, Cornelia Phillips Spencer Papers, #683, SHC; *OR* 49, pt. 1, 324, 331; *OR* 47, pt. 3, 739, 753, 756; Roman, *Beauregard*, 2, 385-387; Chester S. Davis, "Stoneman's Raid Into Northwest North Carolina," (Winston-Salem) *Journal and Sentinel*, October 4, 1953.

14. Hester B. Jackson, ed., *Surry County Soldiers in the Civil War* (Charlotte, NC, 1992), 425-426; *OR* 49, pt. 1, 331; (Salem, NC) *People's Press*, April 6, 1865.

15. *OR* 49, pt. 1, 331-332; Van Noppen, *Stoneman's Raid*, 34; Basil W. Duke, *A History of Morgan's Cavalry* (1867; reprint, West Jefferson, Ohio: 1997), 618; Samuel W. Scott and Samuel P. Angel, *History of the Thirteenth Regiment Tennessee Volunteer Cavalry, U.S.A.* (n.d.; reprint, Don Crow and Harold Lingerfelt, 1977), 263-264, 236.

16. *OR* 49, pt. 1, 331-332; Kirk, *Fifteenth Pennsylvania Cavalry*, 495-496, 497, 499; Van Noppen, *Stoneman's Raid*, 36.

17. *OR* 49, pt. 1, 332; *OR* 47, pt. 3, 769; Claim of Thomas Shelton, #12917, Patrick County, VA, in Record Group 217, Settled Files of the Southern Claims Commission, National Archives, Washington, D.C. (hereinafter cited as SCC, NA)

18. *OR* 49, pt. 1, 332-333.

19. Claim of Sarah Dalton, #3487, Yadkin County, North Carolina, SCC, NA.

20. John W. Fries, "Reminiscences of Confederate days," Fries Papers, NCSA.

21. *OR* 49, pt. 1, 324; Fries, *Forsyth*, 142; Rights, "Salem in the War," 287; (Salem, NC) *People's Press*, May 27, 1865. Fries, "Reminiscences of Confederate days," Fries Papers, NCSA. According to the *People's Press*, the Federals also left a few wounded from the 12th Ohio and 10th Michigan to recuperate in Salem.

22. *OR* 49, pt. 1, 332-334; Jefferson Davis, *A Short History of the Confederate States of America* (New York, 1890), 486; Van Noppen, *Stoneman's Raid*, 42-46; Janet B. Hewett, ed., *Supplement to the Official Records of the Union and Confederate Armies* (Wilmington, 1996), pt. 2, vol. 30, serial #42, 231.

23. Barrett, *Civil War in North Carolina*, 356-357; *OR* 49, pt. 1, 333; Colton, *Column South*, 286.

24. *OR* 49, pt. 1, 333.

25. *OR* 49, pt. 1, 333; Spencer, *Last Ninety Days,* 199; "Stoneman's Raid On Salisbury," Captain A. G. Brenizer Papers, NCSA. According to Spencer, Gardner's force had been disposed "at various points on the road toward Mocksville . . . there being nowhere more than one hundred and fifty men at any point."

26. *OR* 47, pt. 3, 790-791; *OR* 49, pt. 1, 333-334; Warner, *Generals in Gray*, 97-98, 232-233; John C. Pemberton, *Pemberton: Defender of Vicksburg* (Chapel Hill, NC, 1942), 262, 265-266. According to Gillem (*OR* 49, pt. 1, 334) Pemberton commanded Salisbury's artillery, while Pemberton (265-266) claimed only that he "witnessed the capture of our last piece of artillery."

27. *OR* 49, pt. 1, 333.

28. *OR* 49, pt. 1, 333; Scott, *Thirteenth Tennessee Cavalry*, 238.

29. Harriet Ellis Bradshaw, "General Stoneman's Raid On Salisbury," Harriet Ellis Bradshaw Papers, #1444-z, SHC; Jo White Linn, "There Is No Music In My Soul Today," *UDC Magazine*, October 1994, 19-20; Jo White Linn, *The Ramsay Family*, n.p. MS, 1997; Spencer, *Last Ninety Days*, 200, 201; *OR* 49, pt. 1, 325. Beall's account confuses the later action at Yadkin Bridge with the capture of Salisbury.

30. *OR* 49, pt. 1, 324-325, 334; Spencer, *Last Ninety Days*, 200-201, 203; J. E. Newsom, "Stoneman's North Carolina Raid," *Philadelphia Weekly Times*, December 14, 1878. The reports of Gillem and Stoneman differ on what was destroyed in Salisbury. Stoneman's report is followed in the text.

31. Van Noppen, *Stoneman's Raid*, 67-68; Spencer, *Last Ninety Days*, 204; Warner, *Generals in Gray*, 347; "Stoneman's Raid On Salisbury," Captain A. G. Brenizer Papers, NCSA. Despite this failure, the raiders' success in damaging the railroad meant that the flight of the Confederate government would have to depend on horses (Chester S. Davis, "Stoneman's Raid into Northwest North Carolina," [Winston-Salem] *Journal and Sentinel*, October 4, 1953).

32. W. N. Watt, *Iredell County Soldiers in the Civil War* (W. N. Watt, 1995), 99-100; *OR* 49, pt. 1, 334; pt. 2, 446; "Diary Entry for April 14-June 26, 1865," Loula Hendon Donnell Papers, #4206, SHC.

33. *OR* 49, pt. 1, 334, 324; Van Noppen, *Stoneman's Raid*, 71.

34. "Diary Entry for April 14-June 26, 1865," Loula Hendon Donnell Papers, #4206, SHC; Basil W. Duke, *Reminiscences of General Basil W. Duke* (1911; reprint, West Jefferson, Ohio, 1997), 462-465; Duke, *Morgan's Cavalry*, 624. According to Duke, *Reminiscences*, 462, Echols had furloughed his infantrymen before riding southward with his cavalry forces.

35. Duke, *Reminiscences*, 464-465; Duke, *Morgan's Cavalry*, 624, 626.

36. Spencer, *Ninety Days*, 216-217; Barrett, *Civil War in North Carolina*, 362.

37. *OR* 49, pt. 1, 334-335; pt. 2, 446; Warner, *Generals in Gray*, 199-200; "Notes of Stoneman's Raid, in Burke County and the Town of Morganton," 2-6, Cornelia Phillips

Spencer Papers, #683, SHC. Gillem estimated the opposing force at three hundred men (*OR* 49, pt. 1, 334)

38. *OR* 49, pt. 1, 334-335; pt. 2, 446; T. Geo. Walton, "Home Guards Face Stoneman," in Walter Clark, ed., *Histories of the Several Regiments and Battalions From North Carolina in the Great War 1861-65*, 5 vols. (Goldsboro, N.C., Nash Brothers, 1901), vol. 5, 635-636; "Notes of Stoneman's Raid, in Burke County and the Town of Morganton," 5, Cornelia Phillips Spencer Papers, #683, SHC.

39. "Notes of Stoneman's Raid, in Burke County and the Town of Morganton," 8-9, Cornelia Phillips Spencer Papers, #683, SHC; Claim of Margaret Williams, #20171, Burke County, NC, SCC, NA.

40. Barrett, *Civil War in North Carolina*, 363; Vernon H. Crow, *Storm in the Mountains* (Cherokee, N.C., 1982), 127-128.

41. *OR* 49, pt. 1, 335; pt. 2, 446; Emma L. Rankin, "Stoneman's Raid," in *In Memoriam, E. L. R.*, 33, Emma L. Rankin Papers, #621-z, SHC.

42. Barrett, *Civil War in North Carolina*, 364; Warner, *Generals in Gray*, 213-214; "Interview with George Fortune," Civil War Clippings File, North Carolina Room, Pack Memorial Library, Asheville, NC (Hereinafter cited as PML).

43. *OR* 49, pt. 1, 335; Van Noppen, *Stoneman's Raid*, 84.

44. Van Noppen, *Stoneman's Raid*, 89-90; *OR* 49, pt. 1, 335-336; Crow, *Storm in the Mountains*, 128; James M. Ray, "Asheville in 1865," *The Lyceum*, September 1890, copy in Civil War Clippings File, North Carolina Room, PML; "Stoneman's Raid On Salisbury," Captain A.G. Brenizer Papers, NCSA; Scott, *Thirteenth Tennessee Cavalry*, 241.

45. Van Noppen, *Stoneman's Raid*, 109-110; Kirk, *Fifteenth Pennsylvania Cavalry*, 515, 517.

46. *OR* 47, pt. 1, 29.

" I . . . have seen many brave sights, but nothing comparable to this."

The Official Report of Maj. Gen. Henry D. Clayton and a Reminiscence of Col. Henry G. Bunn

Edited by Mark L. Bradley

O f the two Confederate eyewitness accounts of Bentonville reprinted here, the first is a previously unpublished after-action report written less than two weeks after the battle, and the second is a reminiscence that sank into undeserved obscurity after it appeared in the pages of a Raleigh, North Carolina newspaper 110 years ago. These eyewitness accounts were written by two veteran officers of the Army of Tennessee—one a division commander and the other a brigade commander (by virtue of the wounding of his superior officer). The accounts of these two men provide very different perspectives of the same battle.

The Battle of Bentonville, North Carolina, was fought March 19-21, 1865, and was the last major engagement of the Army of Tennessee. That once-mighty host had been virtually annihilated at Franklin and Nashville during Gen. John Bell Hood's disastrous Tennessee Campaign the previous autumn. A bare remnant of 4,500 officers and men took part in the fighting on March 19, by far the bloodiest day at Bentonville.

The Army of Tennessee formed only a part of Gen. Joseph E. Johnston's Army of the South, which consisted of several hastily assembled components. In addition to the Army of Tennessee troops, there were the "Department of North

Carolina" infantry and artillery under Gen. Braxton Bragg, Lt. Gen. William J. Hardee's corps, and Lt. Gen. Wade Hampton's cavalry. These four distinct forces totaled roughly 20,000 effectives on March 19, but due to a combination of bad luck and poor command decisions, many of these troops either did not take part in the battle or were committed only when the outcome was already decided. Moreover, during the final year of the war, the Confederates had been forced to rob the cradle and the grave in order to fill the ranks. The largest brigade in Johnston's army at Bentonville was the North Carolina Junior Reserves Brigade, which consisted almost exclusively of seventeen-year-old boys. It is therefore hardly surprising that the veterans of the Army of Tennessee were called upon to bear the brunt of the first day's fighting at Bentonville.

Those veterans would face a familiar adversary at Bentonville: Maj. Gen. William T. Sherman's grand army, which had battled the Army of Tennessee throughout the Atlanta Campaign. Since leaving Savannah, Georgia, in mid-January 1865, Sherman's "army group" of 60,000 officers and men had been marching in two wings for greater mobility and better foraging prospects. In South Carolina Sherman's front was often forty miles wide, but upon learning in late February that Johnston had assumed command of the Confederate forces opposing his progress, "Uncle Billy" became more cautious out of respect for his wily old adversary. Although Sherman's columns were all within easy supporting distance as they approached their objective of Goldsboro, North Carolina, General Hampton's reports and the faulty North Carolina maps induced Johnston to strike the Left Wing of Sherman's army near Bentonville in the belief that it was separated from the rest of the Union army by more than a day's march. The Confederacy's general-in-chief, Robert E. Lee, had placed Johnston in command with orders "to concentrate all available forces and drive back Sherman." Until now this had been an impossibility. Although the enemy columns were actually closer to each other than Johnston had supposed, the Federal high command had grown so overconfident by the afternoon of March 18 that it supposed all danger had passed.

The commander of the Federal Left Wing, or Army of Georgia, was Maj. Gen. Henry W. Slocum. It was this portion of Sherman's army that would do the fighting at Bentonville on March 19. Since Slocum's wing was nearest the Confederate forces concentrating at Smithfield, Sherman had directed that it march in fighting trim, accompanied only by its ordnance wagons and ambulances. The rest of the Left Wing's wagon train followed the Right Wing several miles to the south, escorted by two divisions. Slocum's remaining four divisions of infantry and the cavalry division commanded by Bvt. Maj. Gen. Judson

Kilpatrick—about 20,000 troops in all—marched on the Old Goldsboro Road toward the trap Johnston had set for them at the Willis Cole plantation two miles south of Bentonville.

Johnston's plan of attack at Bentonville was actually the brainchild of his cavalry commander, Wade Hampton. The plan was simple: one portion of Johnston's army—Hoke's Division of the Department of North Carolina—would block the Goldsboro Road with orders to halt Slocum's advance. While the Federals deployed troops to drive the Confederates in their front, the Army of Tennessee contingent and Hardee's Corps, which were concealed in thick woods, would fall upon the enemy's left flank and roll up the rest of the column. It was an excellent plan, but its execution was hampered by the fact that the Confederates had only one approach route to the battlefield. In Johnston's words, the Southerners' deployment "consumed a weary time."

Our two Confederate eyewitness accounts of Bentonville begin at this point. The first is an unpublished after-action report of Maj. Gen. Henry D. Clayton, who commanded a division in Stephen Dill Lee's Corps (commanded by Daniel H. Hill), while our other eyewitness, Col. Henry Bunn, commanded a brigade in Maj. Gen. Edward C. Walthall's Division of Alexander P. Stewart's Corps (commanded by Maj. Gen. William W. Loring). As we shall see, the denominations of regiment, brigade, division and corps are misleading when assessing the numerical strength of the Army of Tennessee contingent at Bentonville. For example, Clayton's Division numbered only 867 effectives, and Reynolds' Brigade—which Bunn led at Bentonville—mustered fewer than 200 troops. In fact, Stewart's Corps consisted of just 890 officers and men, about the size of an early-war regiment.

As General Clayton tells us, the Federals attacked first, about noon on March 19, and were easily repulsed. We also learn from Clayton that the Army of Tennessee launched its own attack three hours later. The "last grand charge of the Army of Tennessee" was at first a resounding success, but as had so often happened to that luckless aggregation in previous battles, their attack lost momentum and eventually failed due to the blunders of the Confederate high command and the arrival of Federal reinforcements. The March 19 battle thus ended in a bloody stalemate.

The arrival on March 20 of the Federal Right Wing, or the Army of the Tennessee, commanded by Maj. Gen. Oliver O. Howard, gave the Federals a three-to-one numerical advantage over the Confederates. Neither Clayton nor Bunn devote much space to the fighting on March 20-21, although the former notes that one of his brigades was transferred to the extreme left flank on the afternoon of March 21 to assist in the repulse of a Federal XVII Corps division led by Maj. Gen. Joseph A. Mower.

The eyewitness accounts of Clayton and Bunn are very different: the former's report is straightforward and terse, whereas the latter infuses his narrative with numerous incidental details and anecdotes. They provide two unique views of the same battle, and from vantage points that were probably never more than several hundred yards apart. What follows is the Battle of Bentonville as it appeared to Gen. Clayton, followed by the reminiscences of Col. Bunn.

Hd[.] Qrs. Clayton's Division
In the Field[,] 30th March 1865

Major [J. W. Ratchford]:

I have the honor respectfully to report:

On the morning of the 19th inst. this division went into line of Battle near Bentonsville [sic] on the right of the Corps and the Army. This was about 10 A.M. The Division was composed of three Brigades with a total effective as follows: Stovall[']s 323 [officers and men], Jackson[']s 109 & Baker[']s 435.[1] The first two [brigades] composed the front, and the last the rear lines. I deployed skirmishers upon my right and adopted the other usual precautions to protect that flank.

Having been informed that the line would probably be changed[,] I delayed constructing breastworks. Skirmishing in my front becoming very heavy[,] I ordered breastworks to be made. About this time Govan's Brigade went into position on my right.[2]

We had only time to throw together a few rails and logs when a few minutes before 12 o'c[lock], the enemy made a vigorous attack, mainly upon my front, but extending a short distance to my right and left. They were most handsomely repulsed, with a loss of about twenty five killed dead, among them a Major, and a number wounded, with a few captured unhurt. My own loss did not exceed ten killed and wounded.[3]

At 3 PM our lines were advanced to attack the enemy. About five hundred yards in front we came upon the enemy in breastworks, who made only a feeble resistance and fled in confusion. Our line continued steadily to advance about one mile, when after halting a few moments[,] it was ordered forward and to change direction to the left. I then moved forward Baker[']s Brigade, and directed that it should pass Stovall[']s & Jackson[']s Brigade[s], which had now been engaged about one hour. This Brigade continued to advance with spirit[,] driving the enemy in its front with little difficulty. In following it, I found a number of shots from the enemy coming from the right and across its line of march.[4]

I then sent out a few men in that direction and found a line of battle of the enemy only a short distance to the right of the ground over which Baker's Brigade had just passed. I directed that [Lt.] Col[.] [Osceola] Kyle[,] Command-ing Jackson[']s Brigade[,] would deploy what force he could collect from his own & Stovall[']s Brigade in their front and[,] holding them in check[,]secure the rear of Baker[']s Brigade. I found also that either from the greater resistance of the enemy upon the left of Baker[']s Brigade, or from some other cause, his right had swung around further than was desirable. Upon ordering forward scouts and also from an officer of Genl[.] Baker[']s Brigade who reported. . .to us at this time, I learned that the enemy were in force in front of his left. I then asked for help upon Genl[.] Baker[']s left. A portion of Palmer[']s Brigade of Steven-son[']s Division was sent[,] but moved too far to the right, and a portion of it, and also nearly one hundred men of Baker[']s Brigade which fell back about this time[,] passed through the interval made in the enemy[']s line and were supposed to have been captured until two days ago[,] when most of them[,] having marched around the left of the enemy, returned to their commands.[5]

Hastening to collect together my command[,] now somewhat scattered[,] and having reported my position through the staff of the Maj[.] Genl[.] commanding corps, I awaited orders until 10 P.M[.][,] when I was ordered back to my position originally occupied.[6]

Nothing further worthy of mention occur[r]ed during the 20th & 21st, until the evening of the latter day, when I was ordered to send my reserves to repel a demonstration which the enemy had made on the left & rear of our army. Baker[']s Brigade having been sent under this order, I respectfully refer to Brig[.] Genl[.] Baker[']s report.[7]

Herewith I submit [the] report of casualties on the 19th and also of Baker[']s Brigade on the 21st.[8]

I cannot close this report without remarking [on] the uniform good behavior of the Troops and tendering my thanks to Lt. Col. Kyle[,] com[man]d[in]g Jack-son[']s Brigade[,] for the efficient manner in which he conducted the same[,] and also to Lt[.] E[.] C[.] Thornton[,] ADC[,] for his gallantry in capturing a piece of artillery, cais[s]on & horses, as more fully stated by Lt[.] Col[.] Kyle in his Report.[9]

I am[,] Major[,]

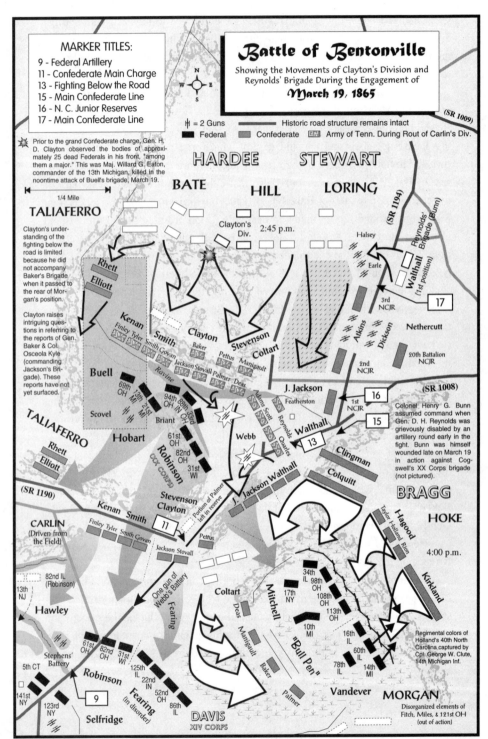

MARKER TITLES:

9 - Federal Artillery
11 - Confederate Main Charge
13 - Fighting Below the Road
15 - Main Confederate Line
16 - N. C. Junior Reserves
17 - Main Confederate Line

Prior to the grand Confederate charge, Gen. H. D. Clayton observed the bodies of approximately 25 dead Federals in his front, "among them a major." This was Maj. Willard G. Eaton, commander of the 13th Michigan, killed in the noontime attack of Buell's brigade, March 19.

1/4 Mile

Clayton's understanding of the fighting below the road is limited because he did not accompany Baker's Brigade when it passed to the rear of Morgan's position.

Clayton raises intriguing questions in referring to the reports of Gen. Baker & Col. Osceola Kyle (commanding Jackson's Brigade). These reports have not yet surfaced.

Battle of Bentonville

Showing the Movements of Clayton's Division and Reynolds' Brigade During the Engagement of
March 19, 1865

(SR 1009)

= 2 Guns   Historic road structure remains intact

■ Federal   Confederate   Army of Tenn. During Rout of Carlin's Div.

Colonel Henry G. Bunn assumed command when Gen. D. H. Reynolds was grievously disabled by an artillery round early in the fight. Bunn was himself wounded late on March 19 in action against Cogswell's XX Corps brigade (not pictured).

Regimental colors of Holland's 40th North Carolina captured by Cpl. George W. Clute, 14th Michigan Inf.

Disorganized elements of Fitch, Miles, & 121st OH (out of action)

Very Respectfully
Your ob[edien]t Servant[,]
H[.] D[.] Clayton[,]
Maj[.] Genl[.]

"The Battle of Bentonville. As Described by Another Eye-Witness—A Native of North Carolina—Now a Distinguished Citizen of Arkansas." By Henry G. Bunn[10]

Raleigh *News & Observer*, July 15, 1887.

Camden, Ark June 9, 1887

Dear Sir: The package of newspapers (*News and Observers*) came last night. You will accept my sincere thanks. Nothing could have interested and gratified me more than the speech of the Hon. Alfred M. Waddell.[11]

The battlefield of Bentonville was in many respects the most peculiar it was my fortune to see during my four years of service. There was an old field extending from north to south, or nearly in that direction, lengthwise. It appeared to be two or three hundred yards wide. It was comparatively free from undergrowth, at least towards the northern end. That end of it seems to have been cleared originally as a sort of recess in an ugly wilderness of black-jacks [a type of scrub oak] and other tangled undergrowth, which still flanked it on the north and west side (for three hundred yards down the west side as far as the dry branch). The southern portion of the field seems to have been originally a great deal wider than in the northern portion. The field must be more than half a mile long from north to south. The widened south end was, at the time of the battle, grown up with old field pines pretty much all over, ranging in diameter from ten inches down.[12]

[Maj.] Gen. [Robert F.] Hoke, of your state, commanded a division numbering about 5,000 men. His right flank rested on the east side of the open and narrow northern end of the field, touching it at a point not more than 150 yards from the extreme northern end, and extending east from thence, his left seemingly a little forward.[13] This division occupied temporary rifle pits at the opening of the battle, which was at 2 p.m. March 19th, 1865.[14] At least that was the hour fixed by orders for the advance upon the Federal army, and I think the orders were promptly obeyed, as all of Gen. Johnston's were, usually.[15]

The next command was [Lt. Gen.] A. P. Stuart's [Stewart's] corps, or rather the advance of it, composed of two very small divisions, one commanded by the late [Maj. Gen.] W[illiam] W. Loring, of subsequent Egyptian fame and a native of your state, and the other commanded by that gallant gentleman, now senator in Congress from Mississippi, [Maj.] Gen. E[dward] C. Walthall.[16]

Gen. Loring's division was to the west of the field, his left resting on the western edge of it near the dry branch spoken of above. His line extended about due west, at least perpendicular to the field. His left was considerably in advance of Gen. Hoke's right on the other side of the field. Originally Loring's position may have been directly opposite (across the field) to Hoke's, but I speak of him as he was when the battle had fairly opened.

Walthall's division had no place in the regular line before the battle began. Or rather I should say that his place was between Hoke and Loring in the open field, but as all the artillery we had occupied that space, General Johnston personally placed Walthall's division just in rear of Hoke's right in the woods of pines and oak trees, some fifty yards, and fronting obliquely to the right so as to march direct to his assigned place in the line—the open field—when the order to advance to battle should be given.[17] While Gen. Johnston was marching the division around the northern end of the field to seek a temporary position for it before the battle, about noon I should say, and just as the division was moving by the flank, going south to its temporary position behind Hoke, it being near the northeast corner of the field, Brig. Gen. D[aniel] H. Reynolds, commanding the Arkansas brigade of the division, had his leg taken off by a cannon ball from the enemy's battery stationed in the south end of the field. The ball struck his horse fairly in the breast and passed out at the left side so as to cut off the General's leg about the knee. The command of that brigade then fell to the lot of the writer, as senior colonel, and this imperfect sketch of the battle is given from memory of the situation as it appeared to him occupying that position, and with no written data to assist.[18]

Gen. John C. Brown, afterwards governor of Tennessee, I think, commanded the advance of Cleburne's old division. Gen. Cheatham, I believe, was also present. [Bunn is mistaken here. Major General William B. Bate commanded the remnant of Cheatham's Corps on March 19, which included Cleburne's Division. Major General Benjamin F. Cheatham did not reach Bentonville until about noon on March 21.] Whether these two were under Stuart [Stewart] or Hardee I do not now remember. Hardee's [Corps], from

Charleston, I think, was on the extreme left. In fact I think these last, owing to some accident, were latest in line.[19]

I think all the artillery of both armies was stationed in the old field; I think we were ordered to advance obliquely to the right in going into battle. . . .Our orders were to advance quickly, so that our left would brush Hoke's right; then he was to advance with us obliquely across the field, driving the enemy's fortified pickets or skirmishers, and having thus crossed that part of the field diagonally, our right should touch Loring's left a few yards in the woods west of the edge of the field.[20] This done, the enemy being strongly fortified . . . the whole line was to assault the works. . . .

As our division was traversing the field between Hoke and Loring, our artillery had gradually to cease its fire as we came in front of the guns, but the fire of the enemy's artillery was simply terrific. Added to this a brisk skirmish fire from behind piles of fence-rails was pouring into us the entire distance. The veteran soldiers of Walthall, scarcely any of them without their quota of wounds and scars, marched in as perfect order as on dress parade, at a quick-step, with bright guns at right shoulder shift . . . through this iron and leaden hail, without firing a gun, until they leaped the rise in front of the Federal works. This passage through the old field was the most magnificent sight I witnessed during the war in the way of cool courage. Gen. Walthall, riding with the writer [and] observing the pageant, seemed for a moment to be carried away with admiration, and pointing to the perfect line, said, "I have been in all, or nearly all, the battles fought by the Army of Tennessee, and have seen many brave sights, but nothing comparable to this." A wounded Arkansan, no longer able to keep pace with his comrades, hobbled up to Hoke's men . . . and heard from these strangers exclamations of admiration and wonder, such as would have turned the heads of the "Old Guard"[21]

Just at the point where Walthall struck Loring, was the dry branch, bordered on the margin nearest us by an immense thicket of briars, and on the south side by an abrupt rise five or six feet high, just high enough to protect us from the enemy's fire, while re-arranging our line, disarranged by the scramble through the briar thicket. Here in this dry branch we found Loring's Mississippians, who it seems had advanced somewhat, but were now hesitating to undertake the ugly work before them. These gallant fellows dare anything, but the situation de-manded a special girding up. I do not remember to have seen during the war a more formidable line of infantry fortifications than that just a few yards in front of us at this time, and behind which was a full line of Sherman's best. Right at this point occurred one of those little episodes, which often during war, accomplish greater results than genius.[22]

The soldiers from nearly every Southern state were dubbed with a nickname during the war. This was originally given at first in derision, but afterwards in many cases became names of endearment. They were generally uncouth in sound, being intended at first to be derisive. Early in the war our neighbors the Texans gave us Arkansans the name of "Joshes," and we in turn called them "Chubs," which is a species of. . .low Mexican. The Mississippians were called "Mudheads"; why, I never knew, for it is a most villainous name for such gallant gentlemen to bear as were those same Mississippians.

Well, about the way Sherman's grand army was boosted out of the breastworks at Bentonville was this. When we had got beside Loring's Mississippians and gotten rid of the North Carolina briars, an Arkansan who doubtless had a keen appreciation of his neighbor's feelings, yelled out to Loring's folks: "Mudheads, ain't you goin'[?]"

"We'll go if you will, Josh."

"All right, here's at ye."

And such another Arkansas yell as there was then! The echoes of it had not died away when we and Sherman's "bummers" were having a half-mile footrace between his abandoned breastworks and the swamps, the "bummers" in the lead. (Sherman's really gallant folks were called "bummers" in those days.) After putting the swampy thicket between us and them, the Federals made a stand when, we were informed at the time, they were reinforced by the two corps from the other road, increasing their number from 35,000 to 70,000, ours being about 15,000.[23] Such was the manner in which Sherman was driven from his works. His line thus having been broken near its center, the remainder of it of course followed immediately and I might say simultaneously. . . .

This is a hasty sketch of the first day of North Carolina's greatest battle during the war, by one of her sons, whose sole object is to tell of the deeds of strangers—his old comrades—done on her soil.

I do not write this for publicity, but to serve as memoranda. If you don't wish to print it you can give it to your Confederate society to be filed away, to be kept until other times and future generations, may as they will, delight to do honor to the finest citizen-soldiery that ever graced the cause of constitutional government. . . .

Yours truly, G. Bunn

*   *   *

On the cold, rainy night of March 21-22, 1865, Johnston's vastly outnumbered Army of the South evacuated its position at Bentonville and retreated
northward eighteen miles to Smithfield, while Sherman's army marched on to
Goldsboro. Contrary to the expectations of Johnston, Sherman and nearly everyone else, the two armies had fought their last major battle at Bentonville.

On April 9 Johnston undertook a thorough restructuring of his army, which
he renamed—to no one's surprise—the Army of Tennessee. The army's consoli-
dation left many officers without a command, including General Clayton. Colonel Bunn, however, was given command of the 1st Arkansas Consolidated, which
consisted of regiments from Reynolds' Brigade. Barely two weeks later, on April
26, 1865, Johnston surrendered his command to Sherman at James Bennett's
farmhouse near Durham Station. It was the largest surrender of the war, involving
roughly 89,000 troops stationed in North Carolina, South Carolina, Georgia and
Florida.

(Editor's note: I wish to thank the William Stanley Hoole Special Collections Library
at the University of Alabama-Tuscaloosa for its generous permission to print this report
from the Henry David Clayton Papers.)

Notes

1. At Bentonville Clayton's Division consisted of Baker's Brigade, commanded by
Brig. Gen. Alpheus Baker; Jackson's Brigade, commanded by Lt. Col. Osceola Kyle;
and Stovall's Brigade, commanded by Col. Henry C. Kelogg. Mark L. Bradley, *Last
Stand in the Carolinas: The Battle of Bentonville*(Savas Publishing Co., 1996), 438.
Hereinafter cited as Bradley, *Last Stand*.

2. Govan's Brigade of Cleburne's Division formed part of the remnant of
Cheatham's Corps, which was commanded at Bentonville on March 19 by Maj. Gen.
William B. Bate. These troops deployed on the right of Clayton's Division. See U. S.
War Department, *The War of the Rebellion: The Official Records of the Union and
Confederate Armies*, 128 vols. (Washington, D. C., 1890-1901), Series I, vol. 47, 1105-
1106. Hereinafter cited as *OR*.

3. Clayton is describing an unsuccessful probing attack launched against his position by Brig. Gen. William P. Carlin's division of the XIV Corps. The attacking force
consisted of six Federal regiments belonging to Bvt Brig. Gens. George P. Buell's and
Harrison C. Hobart's brigades. The slain major Clayton refers to was Maj. Willard G.
Eaton of the 13th Michigan, Buell's brigade. *OR* 47, pt. 1, 449.

4. The Confederate attack actually commenced at 2:45 p.m. The troops routed by Clayton's assault were from Carlin's Division. After Stovall and Jackson had overrun Carlin's position, Clayton ordered his reserve, Baker's Brigade, forward. Baker's Alabamians continued the southerly advance, crossing the Goldsboro Road, where they were fired upon from the right by Bvt. Brig. Gen. Benjamin D. Fearing's brigade of Brig. Gen. James D. Morgan's division, XIV Corps. Ibid., 534-535, 1104-1105.

5. Clayton is referring to Brig. Gen. Joseph B. Palmer's Brigade of Maj. Gen. Carter L. Stevenson's Division, Lee's Corps. Ibid., 1100. The narrative of Clayton's report breaks down at this point, because the general remained near the Goldsboro Road while Baker's and Palmer's brigades plunged into the swampy woodland south of the road. After driving off Fearing's brigade, Baker and Palmer got in rear of the two remaining brigades of Morgan's division, while Hoke's Division was attacking Morgan from the front and right flank (Hoke's left was covered by a virtually impassable swamp). But before Baker and Palmer were able to capitalize on their position, they in turn were attacked from the rear by Bvt. Brig. Gen. William Cogswell's brigade of Bvt. Maj. Gen. William T. Ward's division of the XX Corps, and from the front by elements of Morgan's division. The troops that Clayton refers to in his report as being cut off consisted of seventy men from Palmer's and Baker's brigades commanded by Col. Anderson Searcy of the 45th Tennessee. Searcy's band marched around the left flank of Sherman's army while escorting a dozen Federal prisoners, and reached Raleigh on March 28. Bradley, *Last Stand*, 243-258.

6. Major General Daniel Harvey Hill commanded Lee's Corps at Bentonville. His report of the battle can be found in *OR* 47, pt. 1, 1089-1093.

7. Clayton is referring to an attack launched by Maj. Gen. Joseph A. Mower's division of the XVII Corps against the Confederate left flank near the village of Bentonville. Baker's Brigade was one of several units sent to the left in order to repulse Mower. The Confederate counterattack succeeded, and stemmed a breakthrough that might have resulted in the destruction of Johnston's army by cutting off its only avenue of retreat across a flooded Mill Creek. General Baker's report does not appear in the *OR*, and I have been unable to locate it. Bradley, *Last Stand*, 370-395.

8. The casualty figures Clayton refers to are not enclosed with his report. However, an aggregate total for Clayton's Division appears in D. H. Hill's report. Clayton lost 22 killed, 160 wounded, and 62 missing, for a total of 244 casualties. *OR* 47, pt. 1, 1092.

9. The gun and caisson captured by Lt. Thornton belonged to the 19th Indiana Battery. The Hoosiers lost three of their four guns that day, but later succeeded in hauling off one left behind by the Confederates. The fourth gun was rescued by Pvt. Peter Anderson of the 31st Wisconsin, who received a Medal of Honor and a captain's commission for his heroism. As in the case of Baker's report, Lieutenant Colonel Kyle's report does not appear in the *OR*, and I have been unable to locate it. Bradley, *Last Stand*, 216-218.

10. Colonel Henry G. Bunn commanded the 4th Arkansas, and assumed command of Reynolds' Brigade when its commander, Brig. Gen. Daniel H. Reynolds, was se-

verely wounded at the outset of the battle. Bunn was slightly wounded at the close of the fighting on March 19, and was succeeded by Lt. Col. Morton G. Galloway of the 1st Arkansas Mounted Rifles. The reports of Col. Bunn and his division commander, Maj. Gen. Edward C. Walthall, appear in *OR* 47, pt. 1, 1101-1103, 1104-1105. Bunn's postwar account is far more detailed than either his or Walthall's report, although the latter two documents should be consulted for certain facts omitted in the reminiscence.

11. Bunn is referring to an address made by Waddell entitled, "The Last Year of the War in North Carolina," and which includes an overview of the Battle of Bentonville. A. M. Waddell, *The Last Year of the War in North Carolina, Including Plymouth, Fort Fisher and Bentonville* (Richmond, VA, 1888).

12. Bunn is describing the portion of the Willis Cole plantation that his brigaed traversed during the battle. The narrow northern portion of the field he describes was separated from the wider southern portion by a wooded ravine, which Bunn refers to as a "dry branch." The wider portion continued southward to the Goldsboro Road. Bradley, *Last Stand*, 166-167.

13. The line of Hoke's Division faced west and ran at right angles to the Army of Tennessee's line, which faced south. Hoke's right flank and the Army of Tennessee's left flank met at the northeastern corner of the field Bunn refers to, where two batteries of Hampton's horse artillery were in position. Ibid.

14. The Confederate grand assault was originally scheduled for 2:00 p.m., but was postponed to 2:45 in order to complete some last-minute troop deployments. *OR* 47, pt. 1, 1103, 1105.

15. Unfortunately for the Confederates at Bentonville, Bunn was wrong in stating that Johnston's orders were closely adhered to. General Braxton Bragg commanded Johnston's left wing at Bentonville, and failed to advance as ordered, with ultimately disastrous consequences. Johnston later admitted: "It was a great weakness on my part, not to send him to Raleigh on the 18th [of March]." Bradley, *Last Stand*, 301.

16. At Bentonville Lt. Gen. A. P. Stewart commanded the 4,500-man Army of Tennessee contingent, while Maj. Gen. William W. Loring commanded Stewart's Corps. Loring's two division commanders were Maj. Gen. Edward C. Walthall and Col. James Jackson (who commanded Loring's Division). Bradley, *Last Stand*, 437, 439-440.

17. The Confederates had three batteries in position on March 19. (Several others were present, but apparently saw no action.) There were Hampton's two four-gun horse artillery batteries commanded by Capts. William E. Earle and E. Lindsley Halsey, and a six-gun battery from the 13th North Carolina Battalion commanded by Captain George Atkins. The two horse artillery batteries faced the open field, while Atkins' Battery was on Hoke's line to the left (or south). Ibid., 146-147, 161, 166.

18. General Reynolds' shattered left leg was amputated just above the knee on the afternoon of March 19. He survived his wound, and lived until 1902. Reynolds left a graphic account of his wounding in his diary. Daniel Harris Reynolds Diary, March 19, 1865, Daniel Harris Reynolds Papers, Special Collections Division, University Libraries, University of Arkansas-Fayetteville. Bradley, *Last Stand*, 167, 312.

19. Hardee's Corps began deploying just before noon on March 19, about the time Union general Carlin launched his probing attack. Johnston sent one of Hardee's two divisions—McLaws'—to the left at Bragg's request to aid him in repulsing Carlin's attack. Hardee's other division—Taliaferro's—was sent to the Confederate right. This proved to be Bragg's other blunder of the day, for he actually repulsed Carlin's attack before McLaws went into position. Moreover, McLaws 4,000 troops took no part in the Confederate grand assault, and were only sent in piecemeal at the close of the battle when the outcome was already decided. Nevertheless, Johnston is as much to blame as Bragg, for it was his decision to send McLaws to him in the first place. Ibid., 179-180, 301-302.

20. Bunn is referring to Atkins', Earle's and Halsey's batteries on the Confederate side, and Battery C, 1st Illinois and the 19th Indiana Battery on the Union side. It was one of Battery C's 3-inch ordnance rifles that was responsible for wounding General Reynolds. Ibid., 167-168.

21. This paragraph has been moved from its original location at the close of the article to its proper location in the chronology of events.

22. Bunn is describing the ravine that faced the large open field on the southern portion of Cole's plantation. On the opposite tree line some 300 yards to the west were three partially entrenched regiments of Brig. Gen. James S. Robinson's XX Corps brigade and the four 12-pounder Napoleons of the 19th Indiana Battery awaiting the Confederate advance. It is therefore easy to understand why these veterans of the carnage at Franklin were reluctant to advance into Willis Cole's field. Bradley, *Last Stand*, 205, 216.

23. Union Left Wing commander Slocum actually had 20,000 troops at Bentonville, and Johnston had 16,000. The Federal Right Wing did not reach Bentonville until the afternoon of the 20th, which swelled the Federal numbers to nearly 60,000. The Confederates had roughly 20,000 troops at Bentonville by noon of the 21st. Ibid., 309.

General Joseph E. Johnston's Civil War

A Conversation with Historian Craig Symonds

Interviewed by Mark Snell

T he United States Naval Academy is nestled on the banks of the Severn River at the point where it flows into the Chesapeake Bay. The Academy trains young men and women for future service to their nation as commissioned officers in the Navy or Marine Corps. As a member of the faculty of this historic institution, Professor Craig Symonds teaches midshipmen about that period of American history when classmates at the Naval Academy were forced to decide if they would remain loyal to the Union or cast their lots with the Confederacy.

A California native, Craig received a B.A. from UCLA and an M.A. and Ph.D. from the University of Florida. He served three years on active duty with the Navy, two of them in the Strategy Department of the Naval War College in Newport, Rhode Island. (Craig holds the distinction of being the only ensign ever to lecture at the prestigious College of Naval Warfare.) After another year at the War College as a civilian professor, he began teaching at the Naval Academy in 1976. Craig is a past chair of the USNA History Department, and has been a recipient of the Academy's "Excellence in Teaching Award." He is the author of seven books and editor of seven others. His best-known works are *A Battlefield Atlas of the Civil War* (Baltimore: N & A Press, 1983), *Stonewall of the West: Patrick Cleburne and the Civil War* (Lawrence, KS: University Press of Kansas,

1997), and *Joseph E. Johnston: A Civil War Biography* (New York: W. W. Norton, 1992), which is the subject of the following interview.

*   *   *

MS: What was your impetus to write a biography of Johnston?

CS: Curiosity, I suppose is the best answer to that. I simply was not satisfied with what most of the texts had to say about Joe Johnston as an individual. When I looked at the extant biographies at the time I was considering to undertake the project, I was not satisfied with what I read. I think Gilbert Govan and James Livingood [who wrote *A Different Valor: The Story of General Joseph Johnston, C.S.A.*, published by Bobbs-Merrill in 1956] did a very good job of collecting materials about Joe Johnston and explaining what he did in the war. They did an especially fine job explaining why he had difficulties with Jefferson Davis. But they became such advocates of Johnston—they were essentially defenders of his reputation and his behavior—that I got a sense that I wasn't necessarily getting a full picture. I think it's curiosity as much as anything else that led me to an investigation of Johnston's life. I wanted to satisfy myself that I knew who he was, as well as what he did.

MS: I found your biography to be quite balanced. Sometimes historians tend to "fall in love" with their subjects, or perhaps they set out to vilify them. Did you find yourself leaning one way or the other during the writing of this book?

CS: First of all, thank you for the compliment. Of course, you find yourself leaning one way or another. When you write a biography you have two obligations. One is that you have to try to climb inside the subject himself and see the world as Joe Johnston, for example, saw it. You want the reader to understand the perspective of your subject. That's only half of your job. The other half of your job is to climb outside the skull and take a look objectively at what your subject is doing in the environment in which he finds himself. Often in writing a biography, phase one begins to overwhelm you. You begin to perceive the world the way your subject does. You begin to understand his frustration or his anger or his emotion, whatever it may be. It's not that you become your subject but you certainly become the advocate of your subject.

Craig Symonds conducting a "staff ride" on the Gettysburg Battlefield
for a group of U. S. Naval Academy midshipmen, October, 1997.

Courtesy of Craig Symonds

MS: As if the person about whom you are writing becomes your friend?

CS: Yes—because you haven't finished the biographer's requirement to then
step back and take a look again. The interesting thing about Joe Johnston, as a
subject, is that he carries all his "baggage" with him. I found that in talking about
Johnston to a lot of Civil War Round Tables around the country, that he is one of
two things to most people. He's either the evil scourge that led the Confederacy
down the path to its defeat, the guy who retreated in front of the enemy at every
opportunity, even when he might have inflicted a successful reverse. (Richard
McMurray teases me all the time that Joe Johnston finally would have fought the
Battle of Key West because he wouldn't have had any other place to retreat.) The
other view is that Joe Johnston had the right idea—that his strategy was the one
that the South needed to win the war and had Davis not relieved him and put the
brash John Bell Hood in his place, Johnston's strategy would have worked; it
would have slowed Sherman, Atlanta would have survived through the 1864 fall
election campaign, Lincoln wouldn't have been re-elected, and the South would

have won its independence. So he's either the evil villain for one group or the potential hero for the other group. Of course most of us tend to see ourselves as the heroes of our own experience. The biographer's job is to see the perspective of the subject but then also to step away and look at the reality of that subject's role in the events in which he was participating. I did try very hard to do that and I'm glad you feel I succeeded. I've talked to a lot of people who thought I was much too kind to Joe Johnston.

MS: Really?

CS: If I had been more critical, others would say I was far too critical. I suspect I got it about right.

MS: Since the focus of this issue of Civil War Regiments *is the final campaigns in North Carolina, could you assess Johnston's leadership during this period?*

CS: A very good question. I mentioned the baggage that Johnston brings with him as a historical subject. Johnston also brought a lot of baggage with him to his command of the Army of Tennessee in its twilight days in the North Carolina Campaign. That baggage, of course, was the sore feelings that he had as a result of his confrontations with Jefferson Davis. Davis had made it very clear that he had lost confidence in Johnston and in his strategic vision. Moreover, Johnston had become a participant in what amounted to an internal political cabal against Davis. Finally, Davis thought that Johnston's field command had been found utterly wanting. Johnston knew all these things. When he got the order putting him back in command, he thought Davis had an ulterior motive.

MS: What did Johnston think that Davis had up his sleeve?

CS: He believed that Davis had put him back in command *deliberately* so that he would have to surrender the army, and that the onus of the surrender would land on Joseph Johnston and be a burden he would carry to his grave.

MS: Johnston really believed this?

CS: Yes. That is what he told his wife. It shows to a certain extent how obsessed Johnston had become with his feud with Jefferson Davis. Did he think that Jefferson Davis was so small a man that it was more important to him that Johnston be blamed for the surrender than the fact that the Confederacy was dying? I think he did. Johnston accepted the job anyway, which he believed at least demonstrated his own commitment and dedication. It was only after he accepted command that he learned that Davis had been compelled to appoint him to command by the intercession of Robert E. Lee.

MS: And knowing that Lee interceded on his behalf was important to Johnston?

CS: That changed his mood entirely—that Lee still trusted him, still believed in him, still thought that Joe Johnston could win a victory—meant a lot to him. I think, personally, what Lee believed was that Johnston's name was still a talisman that would have sufficient credibility among the rank and file that the soldiers might return to the flag they had previously deserted, and if nothing else, his reappointment would help restore morale. Johnston then threw himself into the campaign and I think probably did as good a job as he did any place in the war. I suspect this illustrates one other factor about Joseph E. Johnston—he, like most general officers in the war, "grew" in the job. The sad thing from Davis' point of view is that Johnston was asked to do more than he was capable of doing early in the war.

MS: Can you give me an example?

CS: He had to command an army of 70,000-plus troops on the Peninsula at a time when he had never exercised active field command over anything larger than a regiment. He was not prepared for the responsibility. The plan that he wrote for the Battle of Seven Pines proves that. By 1864, and certainly by 1865, he had figured out a lot of things, as had many of his contemporaries, and he was a much better general in 1864 and 1865 than he had been in 1862. I would give him pretty good marks for his North Carolina Campaign. Once you take into consideration all the "degree of difficulty" factors—the circumstance of fighting an overwhelming force with his own force dispersed, and with an army whose morale had been terribly worn down by recent reversals in the field—the way he managed those troops, I think, showed that he was a general who had, if not a sense of genius, which is what his advocates complained, at least a certain amount of competence.

MS: Can you comment on his conduct in the Battle of Bentonville?

CS: I can, though there are others I think more qualified to do that. He was aware that Federals were advancing almost unimpeded through North Carolina. They had a certain amount of disdain by this point for the ability of the Confederates to inflict a serious reversal. Johnston hoped to catch a portion of the enemy with the bulk of his own forces. This, of course, is the tactical objective in almost every campaign you study that Joseph E. Johnston managed. His idea was to bring the larger portion of his own army against a smaller portion of the enemy—this is what he tried to do at Seven Pines, it is what he tried to do at Cassville, and it is exactly what he tried to do, and to a certain extent *did* do, at Bentonville.

MS: It's the principle of mass.

CS: Yes.

MS: Did Johnston's personality affect his generalship at Bentonville?

CS: In a sense, yes. I think Johnston perceived in this opportunity a chance not just to achieve something important in the field to buy time at Richmond for his old West Point-classmate Robert E. Lee, but also the opportunity to demonstrate to those who thought him incapable of offensive action that he could in fact *do* that, that he was not merely "Retreating Joe"—he was "Fighting Joe." It was important to him in his own perception of himself and the perception of him by others that he could fight a battle there. Yet that sad, tragic, forlorn charge of Hardee's elements at Bentonville was the last great hurrah of the Confederate armies. I think he saw something wonderful as well as something tragic in that whole experience.

MS: What was the most fascinating part of this book for you in terms of research and writing?

CS: I think in any biography, one of the most interesting things is finding out how the adult historical figure became the adult that he was. I enjoyed very much learning about the young Joe Johnston—the Joe Johnston that became the man who accepted field command in 1861. Most Civil War scholars tune-in to the Civil War in the 1850s. Perhaps they'll tell you about the difficulties Joe

Johnston had with Jefferson Davis when Davis was Secretary of War and Johnston was seeking confirmation of his promotion to colonel. They might talk about Joe Johnston's resignation from the Old Army. To me, it was fascinating to find out about Joe Johnston the West Point cadet, Joe Johnston the junior lieutenant, Joe Johnston the topographical engineer in Florida, Joe Johnston the Indian fighter in Kansas. Also, I was intrigued by the long-standing friendship and the very rich correspondence that he carried on with George B. McClellan in the early 1850s when they shared talk about conducting a filibustering campaign into Mexico. The whole notion is incredible: Joe Johnston and George McClellan conducting a filibustering campaign to take over part of Mexico and add it to the national domain of the United States! This research gave me an insight into who the young Joe Johnston was, and I think it allowed me to appreciate the adult Joe Johnston—the mature Joe Johnston. It was a rich experience for me to find out who the young man was and how he became the historical Joe Johnston.

MS: You mentioned McClellan's friendship with Johnston. Do you see any parallels between Joe Johnston and George McClellan in terms of generalship?

CS: Well, I noticed you smiled as you asked me that question. Of course, this is a question that a lot of people have addressed. Is Johnston just merely the Southern version of McClellan? There are a lot of things they have in common. They were both beloved of their troops. They were both known as "feeding generals"—they took care with logistics to make sure that the troops were well fed and well shod. They both made sure that they wouldn't commit their forces to battle unless there was a pretty good chance that they would be successful. The troops knew that, and therefore when they *were* committed to battle, they went to battle with some sense of confidence. All of those things are to the good.

MS: But what about the negative correlations?

CS: The problem with McClellan, of course, was that he could not finish. He lost his nerve on the battlefield. You see his nerve breaking down the first time he saw wounded troops after the Battle of Seven Pines. You see McClellan always claiming he's out numbered by as much as two to one, when often the circumstances were just the opposite—he out-numbered the enemy two to one. Stephen Sears suggests that this obsession with being out numbered was a psychological trick McClellan played on himself to avoid having to make a tough decision and commit his army to battle. One important difference between Johnston and

McClellan is that Joe Johnston often *was*, in fact, out-numbered, occasionally by as much as two to one. I don't think Joe Johnston had quite the same difficulty making a tough decision.

MS: But there were similarities.

CS: Yes, there were superficial similarities. Each of them was a sensitive man. Each felt himself a martyr in the position that he occupied—that he wasn't understood by his political enemies, or that his difficulties weren't appreciated. Each leaned heavily on his wife for psychological support. Without doubt there are similarities between the two. I would stop short, however, of saying that Joe Johnston was nothing more than a "Southern McClellan." I think he was a bit more than that.

MS: How has your biography of Johnston changed our perceptions of him?

CS: I don't know. Maybe I should ask you that question. One of the things I did in the year or so after the publication of that book was receive invitations to speak before groups of students of the war, scholars of the war, particularly, of course, the Civil War Round Tables. I found that reactions to the book varied by geography. I mentioned earlier that those who know something about Joe Johnston tend to fall into one of two camps. Either he was the great evil, the great Satan who lost the war for the Confederacy, or the great unsung hero who could have won the war had he not been relieved of command by Jefferson Davis. Each group, I found, cited things that I wrote about in my book to defend its point of view. What I hope I've done in this book is provide a more accurate, a more balanced, sympathetic, and yet not necessarily admiring portrait of Joseph E. Johnston—the "historical" Joseph E. Johnston as well as the "human" Joseph E. Johnston. Who was he in terms of his relation to his wife—how difficult was it for him to go through life having never had a child of his own? What kind of midnight fears did he have, what kind of self doubts did he share? I think understanding the human Joe Johnston as well as the historical Joe Johnston is part of appreciating the role that he played historically.

MS: Will your book affect how we look at the overall conduct of the war?

CS: I'm not entirely sure how it will change the historiography of the war. One of the things I think it's important to understand about the Civil War is that it is more than simply a confrontation between armies on the battlefield. The relationship between Joseph E. Johnston and Jefferson Davis, between Jefferson Davis and his critics in the Confederate Congress, and between those critics *and* Joseph E. Johnston, gives tremendous insight into the inner Civil War of the Confederate government. This was not a case, as many "Lost Cause" students of the war would advocate, of a completely united South fighting with one voice and one will for its independence. This was very much a divided South—in disagreement not just as to means, but even as to ends of what the war was being fought to achieve. Perhaps this book will make some contribution to understanding the internal politics of the Confederacy's war for independence.

MS: What do you think was the high point of Johnston's Civil War career? In other words, during what campaign do you think he displayed his best generalship?

CS: That's a very interesting question. The campaign for which he will always be remembered—and I think *he* would argue was his best campaign—is the Atlanta Campaign. But if you were to ask the other question—what was his *worst* campaign—that's the one that also would be cited most often. It's worthwhile considering that campaign in terms of this dichotomy—I mentioned earlier about his advocates and his enemies. There are two views you can take. First, there is the view that Johnston reported in his own very self-serving memoirs: that he knew exactly what he wanted to do from the beginning of the Atlanta Campaign; to draw Sherman into Georgia, and he would fight only under cover and only when the opportunity gave him the advantage of numbers or circumstance; that he would deliberately draw Sherman away from his lines of supply, making those lines of supply vulnerable and drawing him in—like Napoleon going to Moscow—before he executed this great counter strike that would devastate the enemy. Contemporary evidence suggests to me—and this is one of the things that I say in my book—that he came to this view only after the campaign was about half way through. He was reacting to Sherman; he was not making Sherman react to him. He began to see during the course of the campaign that this could work to his advantage. Maybe some of this is self-justifying, but to a certain extent I also think he was being realistic. He had limited assets. He had a very cautious opponent—Sherman was nearly as cautious in the conduct of that campaign as Johnston was. Sherman only once accepted the tactical offense at Kennesaw Mountain—with obvious results. Johnston began to see that what was happening to him anyway could be turned to his advantage. It was only in the second or third week of May that he began to appreciate this notion—later considered his signature campaign—of drawing the enemy deep into Georgia before launching a counter strike. The difficulty with this campaign is that it can only work if it's allowed to play itself out. And, of course, it was *not* allowed to play itself out.

MS: But what if it had?

CS: The great "what if" question—and all Civil War historians are absolutely obsessed with "what if" questions—is, "What if Jefferson Davis had *not* relieved Joseph E. Johnston?" Would this campaign, subsequently dubbed a kind of Fabian strategy of withdrawl—trading space for time—would it, in fact, have delayed the fall of Atlanta by six to eight weeks, enough to have an impact on the 1864 Presidential Election?

MS: What do you think? Would a protracted campaign to capture Atlanta have affected the outcome of the election?

CS: It's a question to which we'll never know the answer. But it is at least plausible. The reason it never happened was because Joe Johnston had made his greatest error by so alienating Jefferson Davis—by his silly behavior, politically—that the Confederate president had lost all confidence in his field commander and, therefore, took that job away from him, feeling that it absolutely had to be done now or there would never be another chance. The other side of the same coin is, what if—since we're playing that game—what if Jefferson Davis had replaced Joe Johnston *sooner*? What if he had given John Bell Hood an army that hadn't already been depleted of resources and morale, and hadn't already fallen back a hundred miles into enemy territory? Would the tactics that John Bell Hood used have worked better if applied on Rocky Face Ridge than they did on the outskirts of Atlanta? We'll never know the answer to that question either. I think we can be fairly certain of this—that John Bell Hood more likely would have been a success had he been in command from the beginning and Joe Johnston more likely would have been a success if he had been *left* in command until the end. The Atlanta campaign—the final solution to which we will argue about as long as people talk about the Civil War—is, I think, the test of Johnston's strategic vision. It was either brilliant, as his advocates will argue, or absolutely foolish, as his detractors will claim. We will never know.

MS: What if someone other than John Bell Hood replaced Joseph Johnston?

CS: That's a good question. Perhaps William J. Hardee. I've also written a biography of Pat Cleburne, and the one question many people ask me is "What if Pat Cleburne had been put in command of the Army of Tennessee?" I don't think this is a realistic question. Pat Cleburne was never a serious candidate for army command. He had never demonstrated his ability to command a unit larger than a division. As brilliant as he was in command of a division, we cannot extrapolate that to say he would, therefore, have been a great *army* commander. After all, John Bell Hood was a brilliant division commander and we know what *he* did with the Army of Tennessee. But Hardee is a different question. Hardee clearly shared many of the same strategic visions that Johnston did, but that is precisely why he was unacceptable to Jefferson Davis. Jefferson Davis had come to believe that the strategy that Johnston was *allowing* to be played out was simply not going to work, and that a change had to be made.

Jefferson Davis had worked out a code with Braxton Bragg, by which Bragg, who was visiting the Army of Tennessee in July of 1864, would reply by telegraph a series of possible alternatives. First of all, would Joe Johnston agree to change his strategy or was it going to be more of the same? Secondly, if Hardee were to take his place, would Hardee be willing to adopt a more aggressive strategy or would he simply apply the Joe Johnston strategy? Finally, what about John Bell Hood? Bragg, who knew the answer he wanted to give Davis before he even arrived, sent back the coded message indicating that Johnston would *not* change his strategy even though Bragg had never really asked the question. Then he wired that in his opinion, Hardee would be more of the same—even though he had never asked Hardee that question. The best chance of a change of strategy, he told Davis, would be to nominate John Bell Hood for that job. Because Bragg was the one making the effective decision, there was never really much of a chance that it would be anybody but Hood. I guess my short answer is that Hardee would likely have pursued a "Johnstonian" strategy rather than the kind of strategy that became Hood's signature [frontal assaults] in the Battle of Peach Tree Creek, the Battle of Atlanta, and obviously in the Battle of Franklin.

MS: Let's shift to the period after the war. Johnston seemed to have "buried the hatchet" against his enemies rather rapidly. Do you think this may have had any impact on the way he has been portrayed by previous historians?

CS: Maybe. It's a very interesting question. You say his enemies—which "enemies" do you mean?

MS: I mean, his enemies who wore the blue.

CS: Exactly. Johnston's "old enemies," of course, were Jefferson Davis and his crew. He did not bury the hatchet against Davis, nor did Davis bury the hatchet against him. Each of them, in a horribly poignant moment, declined to attend the dedication of a monument to Robert E. Lee for fear that the other would be there and they might have to shake hands. This was many years after the war. It shows how silly and how petty their personal confrontation had become. It's that animosity—the long-standing animosity between Davis and Johnston—that allowed Johnston to be both forgiving of—and forgiven by—his enemies in blue in the years after the Civil War.

MS: Johnston and Sherman seemed to be particularly close.

CS: William Tecumseh Sherman wrote in his memoirs that his most diffi-cult enemy, the one who caused him the most problems in the war and the one he feared the most, was Joseph E. Johnson. It was music to Johnston's ears to hear that. You can almost imagine him waving Sherman's memoirs in Davis' face, as if to say, "See, I was right and you were wrong." So it was much easier somehow for Johnston to forgive, and even be somewhat grateful to, his former opponents in the war who so publicly respected him, just as it was difficult for him to forgive Jefferson Davis for his opposition during and after the war. You know, of course, that when Sherman died his funeral was held in New York on a very bitter-cold, windy afternoon. Joe Johnston was one of the pallbearers. He stood graveside with his hat off in respect to his former opponent, and someone leaned forward and tapped him on the shoulder and said, "General, you must put on hat, you will catch cold." Johnston said, "If I were lying there and he were standing here, he would not put on his hat." And he remained uncovered through the ceremony. He caught a cold which turned into pneumonia, which eventually killed him. Again, a very poignant moment, showing how Johnston in many respects used his former enemies in the field to substantiate his histori-cal reputation as an effective field commander and use it to bludgeon his old political foe, Jefferson Davis, whose hand he would not shake.

MS: I was aware of the fact that Johnston was pallbearer for Sherman but I wasn't aware, until I read the book, that he attended several Union generals' funerals, and was pallbearer to several of them—McClellan, was one of them, I think. There were several that you mentioned in your book.

CS: There were several. Johnston said this in his memoirs, or maybe it was one of the articles he wrote for "Battles and Leaders," the old *Century Magazine* series subsequently published as *Battles and Leaders of the Civil War.* He wrote an article in which he stated that the testimony of one's enemies is the best evidence of one's effectiveness in the field. That clearly is a line he aimed directly at Jefferson Davis.

MS: Since you've already written biographies of Johnston and one of his subordinates, Patrick Cleburne—which has recently been released—one might expect that you would be writing another book about another Western Theater Confederate general. That's not the case, is it?

CS: No, I am currently writing a biography of a Confederate admiral—Franklin Buchanan. A number of my friends wrinkle their brow and say, "Now, who exactly *was* he again?" During the Civil War Buchanan had two moments in the sun. Andy Warhol said everyone gets fifteen minutes of fame. Franklin Buchanan had *two* fifteen minute periods of fame, one of which was in command of the *Virginia*—formerly the *Merrimac*—in the Battle of Hampton Roads. His big moment was not in the fight with the *Monitor,* but during his first sortie against the *Congress* and the *Cumberland.* Buchanan was wounded in that action and had to step aside. Thus he missed the battle against the *Monitor.* He would have a second chance at glory, and that was in command of the *C.S.S. Tennessee* in Mobile Bay against Farragut, on the occasion when Farragut "damned the torpedoes" and steamed into Mobile Bay. One of the interesting things about that confrontation, of course, is that Buchanan was a Marylander—a state that did not secede. Farragut, on the other hand, had been born in Tennessee and spent much of his early life in Virginia, but he nevertheless stayed with the Union. So you had a Southerner fighting for the Union and a Northerner fighting for the Confederacy at Mobile.

In addition to that, Franklin Buchanan is interesting to me because he was also the first superintendent of the United States Naval Academy. He had a long and very distinguished career as a naval officer in the years before the war.

MS: Then I take it your biography will examine his career before the war as well as his years in the Confederate navy?

CS: Yes. I'm going to try to explore both aspects of his life. First, Franklin Buchanan the rising young naval officer and founder of the Naval Academy, the man who was second in command to Matthew Perry in the expedition to Japan. Second, Buchanan the Confederate admiral, an expatriate from his own state, fighting against very long odds on behalf of the small Confederate Navy.

MS: I look forward to reading that. Thanks for the interview.

CS: You're welcome. I enjoyed it.

Book Reviews

The American Civil War: A Handbook of Literature and Research, bySteven E. Woodworth, editor (Greenwood Press, 88 Post Road West, P.O. Box 5007, Westport, CT 06881-5007) 1996. Contents. Appendix. Index. 754pp. $99.50. Hardcover.

Stephen E. Woodworth has filled a major gap in Civil War bibliography masterfully with his work, *The American Civil War: Handbook of Literature and Research.* The Civil War remains the defining event in American history and writers have been refighting it since its end. With as many as 70,000 published works on the war, and with almost one book a day being added, it has become impossible even for professional historians to keep up with the vast amount of literature on the subject. Readers will be pleased to find that Woodworth's work is one of the best bibliographic resources on the war to date.

The *Handbook* is divided into eleven major parts containing forty-seven separate bibliographic essays—each written by a nationally recognized expert. The parts are: General Secondary Sources; General Primary Sources; Illustrative materials; Causation—Events Leading to the War; International Relations; Leaders, Strategy and Tactics: Operations, Campaigns, and Battles; Conduct of the War; The Home Front; Reconstruction and Beyond; and Popular Media.

Each essay begins with a historiographic discussion of the topic and concludes with a bibliography that lists major works relating to it. The essayists are a who's who of Civil War historians. For example, one of the most talented researchers in the nation, T. Michael Parrish, wrote an essay on bibliographies. John F. Marszalek wrote on "Leadership—Union Army Officers" and Grady McWhiney contributed with "Leadership—Confederate Army Officers." Other writers include Judith Lee Hallock, Mark E. Neely, Jr., Anne J. Bailey, and even Gaines M. Foster contributed with a discussion of veterans organizations after the war.

Woodworth's *Handbook* has filled an important gap in Civil War bibliographies that historians and students will find an essential addition to their reference library. This work compliments other, older bibliographic resources, including *Civil War Books: A Critical Bibliography of the Civil War* (4 vols.; 1971-1972), and Garold L. Cole's *Civil War Eyewitness* (1988). A more recent addition has been David J. Eicher's *The Civil War in Books* (1997). This work is a collection of critical mini-reviews of what Eicher considers the most important 1100 books on the war. For Northern studies, Eugene C. Murdock's *The Civil War in the North* (1987) and Michael A. Mullins and Rowena A. Reed's *The Union Bookshelf: A Selected Civil War Bibliography* (1992) are a good place to start. For Southern works see T. Michael Parrish and Robert M. Willingham, Jr., *Confederate Imprints* (1987), and E. Merton Coutler *Travels in the Confederate States* (1947), as well as Richard B. Harwell, *In Tall Cotton: The 200 Most Important Confederate Books for the Reader, Researcher, and Collector* (1978).

Woodworth's *Handbook* is a good starting point for any topic that interests Civil War scholars and students. The work goes beyond covering books, to encompass many other sources. Steven Fisher included an essay on "Unpublished Manuscript Collections," while David Bosse added on "Maps, Charts, and Atlases." The Late Charles Edmund Vetter and Gary Dillard Joiner wrote on "Photographs and Drawings." And there is an entire section devoted to "Popular Media" with essays on film, television, music, and novels that portray the war.

Many of the continuing debates in Civil War historiography are covered in the essays as well. Mark Grimsley's fine essay "Modern War/Total War" traces all sides in the recent debate over whether or not the Civil War was the first modern war. Another good example is found in "Part IV Causation—Events Leading to the War." Eric H. Walther introduces the section with a convincing essay on "Slavery, Race, and Culture." To balance the debate, Woodworth also added essays by Frederick J. Blue on "Constitutional and Political Factors," and James M. Russell on "Economic Factors" that led to the war.

While this work is an outstanding contribution to the field of Civil War bibliography, it is not without flaws. Chief among these are Woodworth's choice of topics. Some major fields of Civil War study have been left out. For example, if the reader is looking for a bibliographic essay covering the literature of the use of black troops by Union and Confederacy, a vast growing field of study, they will be disappointed. James Alex Bagget mentioned a title or two about it in his essay on "Emancipation, Freedmen, and the Freedmen's Bureau," but the topic was too broad for his essay and it certainly deserved more thorough coverage.

The text and index are riddled with typographical errors and misspellings. While it is very difficult for anyone to produce a work of this scale without minor errors, the problems with this work interfere with its utility. For example, if a student wanted to look up works by James I. Robertson, Jr., in the index, they would find some of them listed under Robertson's name and other citations listed in the name of "James I. Robertson, Sr." These errors are minor and could be remedied easily in a second edition. The publication might also consider a way to make this important work more accessible by dropping the $99.50 price tag and issuing a paperback or other less expensive edition.

The outstanding contribution Woodworth has made with this work far outweigh any minor criticisms readers may have. In short, Woodworth has combined many of the most talented Civil War historians and had them produce a series of bibliographic essays in their area of expertise. The result is a valuable addition to the field of Civil War bibliography that no student of the conflict should be without.

Thomas Mays   Fort Worth, Texas

Winning and Losing in the Civil War, Albert Castel (University of South Carolina Press, 937 Assembly St., Carolina Plaza, 8th Floor, SC 29208) 1996. Contents. Preface. Afterward. Notes. 204pp. $29.95. Hardcover.

"I am an old-fashioned historian both in what I write about and the way I write. My purpose is to inform, instruct, and, when appropriate, entertain" (p.xi). So states much published, award-winning Civil War historian Albert Castel in the preface to this collection of fifteen of his essays. Together, Castel's mixed bag of previously published articles (1963-1994) plus three first-time essays—including one which originated as a graduate seminar paper in 1951—constitutes an interesting package that reflects his various avenues of research and resultant conclusions on several topics associated with the Civil War.

Organized into four parts—"The Probable versus the Inevitable," "Setting the Record Straight," "How the Civil War Was Fought," and "Of Women and War"—the contents of this volume takes readers in several directions. The following are some salient examples. In the first essay, Castel addresses the question of the inevitability of Union victory and answers that the North could have lost the war. In another offering he argues that regardless of vehement Southern denials, there was indeed a massacre of black Union Soldiers at Fort Pillow in 1864. He also republishes his 1970 defense of Robert E. Lee's military strategy against the criticism of historian Thomas L. Connelly. However, in doing so, he does note that the South ultimately would have fared better without Lee's leadership, for the redoubtable Lee's successes forestalled a far earlier Union victory which would have spared the defeated region much death and destruction. Castel also takes aim in another essay on the historical correctness of Margaret Mitchell's famous novel *Gone With The Wind*, and finds it filled with inaccuracies, which he lists and explains page-by-page. In yet another vein, Castel writes about the important uses of mules in the war. From still a different perspective of inquiry, Castel looks at the little known Civil War story of the divorce of Stonewall Jackson's sister, Laura Jackson Arnold, who was not only a Union supporter in West Virginia but also accused of committing adultery with Union soldiers. And, as might be expected, Castel includes pieces on william Clark Quantrill and the conflict in Kansas and Missouri, and on the Atlanta campaign of 1864 and William Tecumseh Sherman—subjects about which he has written well-received books. On these latter topics, he not only examines various aspects of their importance, but in the case of Sherman, exposes the biases and possibly purposeful errors of fact in Sherman's *Memoirs*. The aforementioned are just some of the topics Castel discusses in this collection.

In all, Castel has put together a group of his writings which, as he stated in expressing his purpose as a historian, inform, instruct, and entertain. In introducing his essays, Castel takes the opportunity to recount the background and to express the meaning of each as a piece of Civil War scholarship. In an Afterward to this collection, Castel offers a few instructive remarks on how to achieve originality in civil War research and publishing. Toward that end, he submits a list of six directions future Civil War historians might follow in their endeavors. In the main, he suggests that rather than "seeking an elusive originality of interpretation of the Civil War, historians should concentrate on...'setting the record straight'" (202). castel believes old stories should be re-evaluated and expanded, important characters and events be compared and packaged in a new context, minor events or lesser known persons be researched thoroughly, arguments be made against poorly supported but accepted viewpoints, and major subjects undergo more research and receive more explication. There are, Castel concludes, still "opportunities for making major contributions to the history of the Civil War" (203).

Albert Castel's own distinguished publishing record has exemplified those injunctions, and *Winning and Losing in the Civil War* is just his latest testimony to his personal practical professional suggestions. Castel declares that these writings "represent most of the best that I have been able to do during four decades of writing articles about America's favorite war" (xi). Consequently, those who enjoy reading well supported scholarly probing into a variety of both well known and esoteric Civil War topics by a noted, and at times unabashedly opinionated, historian, should find this book engaging.

Thomas Burnell Colbert   Marshalltown Community College

The Alabama and the Kearsarge: The Sailor's Civil War, by William Marvel (University of North Carolina Press, P.O. Box 2288, Chapel Hill, NC 27525-2288) 1996. Contents, Appendices, Notes, Bibliography, Index, Maps, Illustrations. 337pp. $34.95 Hardcover.

This book would have been better titled *The Documented History of the Alabama.* The story of the Confederate ship *Alabama* is told with original muster rolls, logbooks, diaries, letters, and census and pension information to cover its historic role from its commissioning to the fateful confrontation with and subsequent defeat by the *U.S.S. Kearsarge.* While Marvel also provides a comprehensive and interesting background on the *Kearsarge,* it is boring compared to his descriptions of the action, engagements, and activity on board the *Alabama.*

Marvel's details of daily life on the raider *Alabama*—with the monotony, tedium, and discomfort of life aboard ship—contrasts with her many engagements and port visits, desertions, and drunken episodes of the crew. Without communication from Jefferson Davis and with no provision for replenishment, the *Alabama* was little more than a piracy vessel. Foreign countries contributed to the *Alabama's* free-spirited, raider mentality by allowing it to challenge all shipping using fraudulent flags of friendly countries to close within firing range before running up the Confederate Stars and Bars.

As the book jacket states, this book "illustrates the drama of the American Civil War on the high seas." The *Alabama* cruised the southern Atlantic for twenty-one months, traveled over 75,000 miles, relied upon its own resources and foreign ports for fuel and ammunition, and was successful in destroying or capturing more than $6.7 million of prize vessels. The captain, Commander Raphael Semmes, was the most successful of all the Confederate naval officers, sinking fifty-five ships—although many of them were considerably smaller and not well armed.

For the nautical enthusiast, this book will fill gaps, particularly for day-to-day events and the tempo and times of the way it was at sea from August 1862 until June 19, 1864. Chapter 19, titled "The Rendezvous," tells of the *Alabama's* final battle off the coast of Cherbourg, France, with Semmes stripped to his skivvies going down with the ship. He and 108 survivors were subsequently rescued.

The author concludes that the *Alabama's* major contribution was its effect on Southern morale, perhaps offering "false hope of victory at sea" and "spreading sympathy" for the Confederacy. Perhaps with thirty other *Alabama's*, the South would have been successful.

Jerry Benson   Captain, USNR-RETLofkin, Texas

Shiloh: The Battle That Changed the Civil War, by Larry J. Daniel (Simon and Schuster, Simon and Schuster Bldg., 1230 Ave of the Americas, New York, NY 10020) 1997. Maps. Notes. Bibliography. Index. B&W Photos. 430pp. $26.00. Hardcover

Shiloh, the Old Testament Hebrew word for "place of rest," became the final resting place for thousands of Americans in 1862. This first large battle of the Civil War killed more men than the cumulative wars in this nation's history up to that date. Much has been written about this battle and now Larry Daniels' work adds to the never-ending volumes of America's tragic era. One wonders what more remains to be discovered about this early 1862 engagement.

The author's main thesis, as the title suggests, is that the Battle of Shiloh was significant, not so much by what the North achieved but by what it denied the Confederacy in winning the war in the West. It was the culmination of Gen. Albert Sidney Johnston's supreme effort to crush Gen. U. S. Grant's army and win back the Mississippi Valley and Tennessee. That the Southern plan almost succeeded, and why it did not, is related here in detail.

It was Daniel's intention to show that the battle could not be viewed apart from the political dynamics behind the scenes in Washington D.C. and Richmond, Virginia. He succeeds in showing the power-posturing between Secretary of War Edwin M. Stanton and Gens. Henry Halleck and George McClellan over what strategic policy should be pursued in the West. Ultimately, it was President Abraham Lincoln's call, and he allowed Gen. Don Carlos Buell to move independently—with almost disastrous consequences. In Richmond it was President Jefferson Davis, according to Daniel, who was culpable for underestimating the numbers and problems that faced by his old friend Johnston. The author claims that the biggest problem in the Confederate west was leadership.

Eventually, the opposing generals and forces positioned themselves in dangerous proximity to each other, inviting an inevitable collision. Once the Confederate leaders decided to concentrate their scattered forces at Corinth, Mississippi, with the intention of striking Grant before he could be joined by Buell, a major battle was all but certain. That Confederate intelligence of Federal intentions appears to have been better served than vice versa is played down by Daniels. Nor, does he give due credit to the Herculean task of concentrating men and logistical support at Corinth from all over the Confederate West, a concentration that allowed Johnston to strike first. Why Grant deployed his forces so haphazardly at Pittsburg landing in the face of a gathering enemy remains unanswered.

It is to Daniel's credit that the coverage of combat on those three days is the most complete this reviewer has seen. He locates and follows in detail every brigade (and most of the regiments), what they were doing, and how they fared in the struggle. While on occasion this micro-approach is confusing for the reader, Daniel does a good overall job describing the ebb and flow of the battle. One feels that he is eye-witness to every crossroad and field simultaneously, and that practically every shot fired is accounted for. The ground vibrates beneath the reader's feet with cannon fire, and the air reeks with the smell the smoke. So engrossing are the battle scenes that one feels entitled to veteran's benefits upon completion of this book. A series of excellent situation maps are of tremendous help in keeping the reader abreast of battle developments.

Daniel examines the commanders on both side in substantial detail and spares no one when it comes to relating their numerous mistakes and blunders. While the North initially basked in the news of victory, the population soon questioned Grant's conduct in the campaign, including his absence from the battlefield at the time of the attack, and his failure to fortify his encampment. Criticism, both official and in public circles, was so loud it is a miracle he escaped being relieved. Only one public person saw in him a rare tenacious quality that the nation could not afford to lose: President Lincoln.

The author castigates both Gens. Johnston and P. G. T. Beauregard for serious leadership faults. While Johnston was the commander, it seems that Beauregard influenced most of the decisions, and this divided leadership caused command and communication problems. From the complex battle order to the tactical execution, things went wrong. Johnston's abandonment of his plan in the middle of the first day's battle by shifting pressure from one flank to the other was a crucial error. In spite of the confusion, mixing of units, and mistakingly firing on their own troops, the Confederates won a tactical victory on the first day. (It is interesting to note that Daniel contends the effect of General Ruggles' hub-to-hub artillery bombardment of the Hornet's Nest has been overstated in that General Prentis was about to collapse anyway.)

Until his dying day Jefferson Davis believed that the war in the West was lost with the death of Albert Sidney Johnston at Shiloh. The author contends that Johnston's army had lost much of its momentum at the same time Grant was establishing a second line of defense. By the time Buell's leading elements reached the field and Lew Wallace finally found the battle, contends Daniel, the likely of crushing Grant's army passed. Unlike many writers, Daniel concludes that Federal reserves scattered throughout the upper South would have prevented the Confederates from reoccupying the Mississippi Valley and Tennessee even if they had been successful.

The author's narrative style flows smoothly, the book is well researched and convincingly argued. Whether he settles the "ifs, ands, and might have beens" to the satisfaction of students of this battle is conjectural. But, there can be little doubt that Daniel ranks high among living authorities on this subject.

Robert W. Glover   Tyler, Texas

Lincoln's Abolitionist General: The Biography of David Hunter, by Edward A. Miller, Jr. (University of South Carolina Press, 937 Assembly St., Carolina Plaza, 8th Fl, SC 29208) 1997. Contents. Bibliography. B&W Photos. Maps. Index. 293pp. $29.95. Hardcover.

Almost everyone has heard of "Black Dave" Hunter, both for his zeal in prematurely freeing and then recruiting slaves into the Union army, and his supposed devastation of the Shenandoah Valley. Few actually know much about the man, his private attitudes, or his other Civil War activities. Edward A. Miller's recent biography of this important Federal general, the only full, scholarly treatment ever accorded Hunter, seeks to correct that oversight—and is quite successful in doing so.

Utilizing all the appropriate primary and secondary sources available, the author, a former U.S. Air Force Academy history professor, has written a comprehensive biography of David Hunter's long and significant military career. He deals with his West Point experiences and his participation in early Trans-Mississippi expeditions, as well as his disillusionment with the army and attempt to create a successful civilian life for himself and his family prior to the Civil War. Thereafter Hunter returned to the Regular Army and the Civil War broke out.

David Hunter was a senior officer and middle-aged when the war began, and Miller effectively brings out the course Hunter followed not only in developing his own antislavery views, which were rare within the officer corps, but in ingratiating himself with the Lincoln Administration. Hunter actually commanded a rag-tag force guarding Lincoln and the White House during the war's early days, cementing his position as an "insider" and developing close associations with the president and key cabinet officers. He used those relationships for his own purposes throughout the Civil War, or at least attempted to do so.

The author details Hunter's unintended banishment to the West, along with his continual letter-writing and carping about being in a sideshow theater when the real war was being fought in the East. Of great interest is the clear picture provided of Hunter's first major command along the eastern seaboard and off-shore islands, as well as the general's revolutionary proclamation of freedom for the slaves of the region. Hunter's disappointment during the spring and summer of 1862, when those freed men failed to enlist in the regiments he created for them is developed, as is the commander's often marginally acceptable military expertise and McClellan-like whining in planning and carrying out operations within his department.

The author's major theme is the disillusionment and gradual distancing with which the Lincoln Administration inevitably came to view Hunter. Even though relieved from his southern command in mid-1862, the author shows that Hunter's progressive views may have influenced Lincoln in formulating emancipation policy before the end of that year. The favorable light in which that influence may have placed Hunter dimmed quickly, however, as he was placed in command of Federal forces in the Shenandoah Valley during early and mid-1864. Miller effectively describes the flaws in Hunter's military abilities, especially those regarding logistics and tactics, as well as his lapses in effective command that led to hatred of him among the rebellious residents of the upper Valley. Finally, the Administration tired of Hunter's excuses and demands for reinforcements and replaced him with a much more effective commander, Phil Sheridan. The author develops this decline in the fortunes of Lincoln's abolitionist general quite effectively.

This is a well written and thoroughly researched biography that deserves a place in the library of any Civil War reader.

Don. E Alberts   Rio Rancho, New Mexico

Matt W. Ransom, Confederate General from North Carolina, by Clayton Charles Marlow (McFarland & Company, Inc., Publishers, Jefferson, NC 28640) 1996. Notes. Bibliography. Index. Maps. 190pp. $24.50. Hardcover.

This book is testimony to the long-term interest that the author developed in the life and Civil War career of a fellow North Carolinian, Matthew Whitaker Ransom. Over the years Marlow sought out obscure sources and tracked down manuscripts in private hands. Regrettably he was not to see the fruit of his effort in print, for he died while the book was in production, which may explain the number of minor errors which made it into print.

Marlow's first chapter is dedicated to tracing the development of the Secession crisis in North Carolina, and in the following chapter Ransom makes his appearance as a young man from a well-to-do planter family of Whig persuasion. Ransom was a student at the University of North Carolina in the 1840s, and a rival for class honors with another young Carolinian who would wear a Confederate general's star—James Johnston Pettigrew. In 1852, when only twenty-six years old, Ransom was elected attorney-general by the state legislature.

An opponent of secession before the bombardment of Fort Sumter, Ransom was sent as a delegate to Montgomery, where he witnessed the birth of the Confederacy. Once war came to the Old North State, Ransom threw himself into the conflict; he soon commanded a regiment of North Carolina infantry, in the brigade of his younger brother, Robert, a West Point graduate. In the first months of war Ransom served in his own state, which was threatened by seaborne invasion. In the spring of 1862 Ransom's unit was sent to Virginia, and he was seriously wounded at Malvern Hill. Sent home to recover, he rejoined his regiment for Antietam, then continued his convalescence at home. Inheriting his brother's brigade, he served again on the coast, then in Virginia, where he was wounded again, this time at the Second Battle of Drewry's Bluff. He was back for the fighting around Petersburg in the fall. The book ends with Appomattox, with only brief reference to Ransom in the post-war era.

This book is a sincere effort to draw out of the shadows a little-known figure whom the author obviously admires. The attempt is only partially successful, and one suspects that the basic reason is lack of sources. No more than half a dozen of Ransom's letters are cited in the text. For pages at a time the author recounts battles and campaigns in which the general had no role, or the activities of his command while he was at home recuperating. All of this is smooth and easy reading, but one has the impression of undue digressions; there is a five-page excursus on the campaigns of William T. Sherman, with whom Ransom never had to contend, this being inserted as "news from other fronts."

The reasons for the author's admiration of Ransom do not come through well. His military career, from what can be seen of it, was unexceptional. Nor is it easy for a reader to warm to the general's character, which seems to have been both frosty and thorny. After one reads that Ransom's personal friends were "limited in number and, almost invariably persons of high social and official rank," and that within his family circle "no trespassers were allowed," it takes a leap of faith to believe with the author that "this aloofness must not be construed as snobbery."

Lee Kennett   University of Georgia (Emeritus)

The Darkest Days of the War: The Battles of Iuka and Corinth, Peter Cozzens (University of North Carolina Press, P.O. Box 2288, Chapel Hill, NC 27515-2288) 1997. Contents. Notes. Appendix. Illustrations. Index. Bibliography. Maps. 337pp. $39.95. Hardcover.

Peter Cozzens has established himself as a skilled writer of Civil War campaign histories. His previous studies include books on Stones River and Chickamauga, works that are notable not only for the attention given to important western battles but also for the author's masterful incorporation of manuscript materials. Cozzens is a meticulous researcher who examines battles from several levels and perspectives. He simultaneously explores questions of strategy and leadership without losing sight of war's horror and irrationality. His newest book, *The Darkest Days of War: The Battles of Iuka and Corinth,* further bolsters his standing as an impressive scholar of Civil War campaign histories.

But why choose to write about Iuka and Corinth? These two little-known engagements occurred in northern Mississippi during late in the summer and early in the fall of 1862. Although this campaign was part of the Confederacy's overall plan to raid into the North, events in Kentucky and Maryland traditionally have overshadowed it. Sandwiched between bloody Shiloh and the siege of Vicksburg, the battles of Corinth and Iuka have been little more than footnotes to the larger Civil War narrative. Only a handful of writers have devoted serious study to this topic since the war ended.

Peter Cozzens agrees, and it is partly due to this obscurity that he devotes an entire book to their study. *The Darkest Days of War* shows how the stories of lesser known engagements can tell us a great deal about leaders, strategy, subsequent battles, and the nature of Civil Warfare in general.

Cozzens describes Iuka and Corinth in small detail, but also seeks larger lessons. His extensive use of soldiers' letters and diaries shows men in the ranks, many of them veterans of Shiloh, aghast by the battles' viciousness, gore, and seeming senselessness. Both armies fought with reduced or depleted supplies to near exhaustion. He emphasizes horrific sights, sounds, and smells violent death creates. His text follows regiments such as the 11th Ohio, which performed so remarkably at Iuka that Confederates refused to take prisoners and instead let survivors of the broken battery go free.

Cozzens also vividly depicts the leading players of this campaign, several of whom were distracted by personal concerns and bruised pride. Ulysses Grant was smarting from his post-Shiloh treatment by the distrustful and jealous Henry Halleck. Casting about for reassurance of his authority and position, he was rumored to be drinking again. His health was poor, and his leg was injured by a freakish fall from a horse. This campaign proved a personal and professional turning point for the future commander of all Federal armies. Doubts and gossip similarly surrounded Confederate General Earl Van Dorn. Van Dorn was reeling from his defeat at Pea Ridge and stories of his philandering multiplied. Both men entered the campaign with personal and professional demons. Grant emerged triumphant, but the impulsive Van Dorn squandered his best chance to prove himself at Corinth; a jealous husband shot the general in the head the following year. William S. Rosecrans also rose to prominence in northern Mississippi. Impatient, brooding, and sensitive, Rosecran's relationship with Grant soured after Iuka and Corinth. Cozzens finds fault with both men, chiding Rosecrans for his touchiness and Grant for his gullibility.

This study affirms that at these minor engagements, as in so many Civil War battles, clashing egos, confused orders, abusive drinking, faulty maps, and unforseen delays were the norm. He reminds readers that maintaining any sort of control of such large-scale violence was extremely difficult and frequently impossible. Battles often took on a life of their own, thrusting helpless humans into a destructive and sprawling explosion of energy and violence. Other times, individual actions can be powerful enough to slow and alter a battle's momentum. At Iuka, for example, the sudden death of Confederate Brigadier General Henry Little so stunned fellow officers that Confederates lost the initiative to deliver a crucial attack. Throughout his book, Cozzens documents numerous examples of how combat can both numb and intensify a myriad of human emotion.

The author's writing style is brisk and tight, yet dense with detail. He evenly mixed thoughtful analysis with narrative. Maps and photographs of major players are well placed in the text, lending visual images to the author's written descriptions. Only occasionally does his penchant for particulars leave the reader overwhelmed.

Determined and patient readers, though, will close the book feeling satisfied. Cozzens successfully demonstrates that these two traditionally ignored battles were important and their study insightful. The South's defeat in northern Mississippi compounded Braxton Bragg's reverses in Kentucky and Robert E. Lee's retreat from Maryland. The Confederacy lost two railroad junctions with vital links to the upper Trans-Mississippi; Chattanooga, Tennessee, and a critical supply base for campaigning in western Tennessee was gone. In addition, Grant's path to Vicksburg was now an easier one to travel. But even for the Federals, inter-command squabbles, hesitancy, and failure to destroy Van Dorn's army, made Iuka and Corinth seem like dark days. Northerners quickly forgot these bleak times when the sun began to shine on their efforts to defeat the South.

Lesley J. Gordon   Murray State University

Richmond during the War: Four Years of Personal Observation, Sallie Brock Putnam (University of Nebraska Press, 327 Nebraska Hall, Lincoln, NE 68588-0520) 1996. Contents. 389pp. $16.95. Paperback.

Ashes of Glory: Richmond at War, Ernest B. Furgurson (Alfred A. Knopf, Inc., 201 East 50th St., New York, NY 10022) 1996. Contents. Notes. Sources. Index. Illustrations. 421pp. $30.00. Hardcover.

Readers of *Civil War Regiments* are certainly familiar with the often quoted phrase "On To Richmond." It was used as a rallying cry by Northern newspapers to inspire the Union Army in its drive to seize the newly established Southern capital in Richmond, Virginia. Clearly the South's most important city at the time of the Civil War, Richmond is the focal point of two recent books. The first, *Richmond During the War*, is the reprinted memoirs of Sallie Brock Putnam. A member of a socially prominent family, Putnam, who married Richard F. Putnam seventeen years after the war, moved to Richmond in 1858 at age thirty-two.

The country was in turmoil over the slavery issue and Sallie saw her Southern way of life threatened by Northern intrusion. Prior to the attack on Fort

Sumter, she claims that "up to this time, we had scarcely begun to realize that war was inevitable. We had hoped against hope" (23). But war did erupt and Richmond was never the same. During her "Four Years of Personal Observation," the reader enthuses over Putnam's euphoria at the onset of secession with words such as "patriotism" and "spirit" immersed throughout her dialogue. Eventually her enthusiasm dissipates as unpleasant sacrifices on all levels of Richmond society began to take their toll. Many of Richmond's women were forced to sell precious belongings for the war effort, as well as seek employment among the offices of the War Department. These jobs normally were reserved for men and Putnam recollects the "the most high-born ladies of the land filled these places as well as the humble poor; but none could obtain employment under the government who could not furnish testimonials of intelligence and superior moral worth" (175).

Putnam was a keen observer of the Northern military campaigns that continually thrust at Richmond. As the Union Army attempted its first direct assault on the city during George B. McClellan's Peninsula Campaign, Sallie recalled that "there never was a period of more alarming excitement than this in Richmond during the entire war, until the time of the ultimate evacuation of the city" (129). With great interest she followed the battles in both the Eastern and Western theaters and is not shy about expressing her view of the generals fighting in the field and the politicians conducting the war from the capital.

The Confederate army had an enormous influence on the city and its daily activities. Putnam recalls waking up to reveille and going to bed at the sound of taps. With the army came the wounded, who stretched the city's hospitals beyond their limits. Unfortunately, the same army that could not prevent the overpowering Union forces from conquering the Confederate capital. Sallie's last few chapters reveal melancholy and bitterness. This was echoed by most citizens of Richmond as their beloved city was abandoned by its leaders and turned to rubble. Exceptions were the free blacks and slaves who rejoiced at the sight of Union Soldiers inhabiting the fallen city.

The most recent edition of Putnam's memoirs are introduced by historian Virginia Scharff, who asserts that "Brock's story is most compelling when she tells us about the physical details of life in Richmond, and offers sharp psychological insight into the state if mind of confederate stalwarts on the home front" (XIX). Scharff correctly exposes a bit of naivety in Putnam, who refuses to believe that Southerners fought the war over the issue to protect slavery. "Instead, she avows. . .that all she and other Southern patriot wanted was peace and liberty, the right to self-determination and freedom first claimed by Virginians like George Washington" (XIX).

Richmond during the War will appeal to a wide ranging audience. Historians and casual readers will appreciate the experience of the war through Sallie Brock Putnam's perspectives. Although Bison Books is commended for making the memoirs available to a general audience, the publisher could have take it a step further. An index and a selection of wartime Richmond photographs, other than the common image of the city in ruins that is reproduced on the cover, would make the book more appealing.

Ernest "Pat" Furgurson's latest work, *Ashes of Glory*, makes full use of memoirs such as Sallie Bock Putnam's—as well as a number of untapped manuscripts. Furgurson, the author of *Chancellorsville 1863*, has produced a social and military history of Richmond. Although the capital of the Confederacy has served as the background in a number of recent books on the war's final campaigns, not since Alfred Hoyt Hill's classic *The Beleaguered City* (1946) has a full-length narrative of Richmond during the Civil War been written. As we learned from Sallie Brock Putnam, Furgurson reiterates that Richmond was much more than just the seat of the Confederate government.

Prior to the Civil War the city thrived on its strong industrial capacity, most notably the Tredegar Iron Works. Primarily for this reason the Confederate States moved their capital there from Montgomery, Alabama. It also helped that Richmond was situated within 100 miles of Washington, D.C. With the Confederacy making Richmond its seat of government came the cold reality that Virginia would become the major battleground of the war and its capital the most sought after prize for the North.

The author points out the diverse ethic backgrounds that made up Richmond's population. A third of the population was black, but there were also large contingents of Irish, German, and a surprising number of Jewish residents. Many of these immigrants were pro-Union, which makes *Ashes of Glory* an intriguing story. One such case was Elizabeth Van Lew, a member of a wealthy and cultured Northern family who prospered in Richmond. According to Furgurson, "before the war was over, almost all of that family fortune would be spent on the Union cause" (77). Van Lew put her own life in danger by performing espionage for the Union and aiding their escaped prisoners. Although her story is intriguing, she was only one of many anti-Confederates living and working in Richmond. The weakest aspect of this book is when Furgurson attempts to describe the unsuccessful Union efforts to take Richmond before the Petersburg Campaign. The book glosses over Northern failures, such as the fiasco at Drewry's Bluff and the disastrous assault at Cold Harbor.

Despite the hardships brought on by the constant threat of the enemy capturing the city, there was adventure and opportunity in Richmond. One such example was the New Richmond Theater constructed thirteen months after its predecessor burned to the ground. The theater's clientele included "the mob, thousands of transients, soldiers, and speculators who were out for amusement" (182). Not all of Richmond's population could afford to be socially active. A Union blockade off the Atlantic Coast caused a shortage of food and other goods that resulted in high inflation. Some took advantage of the situation, such as "sellers of items unaffected directly by the blockade, even farmhands selling scrawny chickens, used it as an excuse for jacking up prices" (191). But Furgurson claims "about one hundred Richmond Jews-a higher percentage than among their coreligionists national, North or South-served in the army" (191).

Besides being a good social history, *Ashes of Glory* is a fun read. Furgurson's narrative flows with quotes and anecdotes about spies, War Department bureaucrats, slaves, and entrepreneurs. As Furgurson points out, "Richmond was not the largest city in the South...But political transients and seasonal society made it bigger and more worldly than official figures suggested" (5).

One minor quibble with the author's writing is his habit of subdividing each chapter. In some cases it is difficult to determine how one section of a chapter relates to another. The impressive list of sources and fine selection of photographs make *Ashes of Glory* one of the better Civil War studies produced in recent years.

Mitchell Yockelson   National Archives and Records Administration

Old Glory and the Stars and Bars: Stories of the Civil War, edited by George William Koon (University of South Carolina Press, 937 Assembly Street, Carolina Plaza, 8th Floor, Columbia, SC 29208) 1995.Introduction. Notes. 228pp. $34.95. Hardcover.

The American Civil War produced a deluge of storytelling. It runs almost as strong today as it did over a century ago. In this anthology, Professor George William Koon of Clemson University analyzes the conflict, one of the most important events in the history of this country, utilizing a particular literary form—the short story.

Koon has chosen sixteen stories for this anthology. He states: "With them, though, I have tried to present with plain good reading a variety of perspectives and tones in Civil War short fiction" (1). To do this he has chosen a mix of works by both familiar and relatively new authors. It includes battle scenes as well as tales of the home front and the influence of the war beyond 1865. It includes recent work by writers such as Robert Morgan, Fred Chappell, and Barry Hannah. Readers will find bits of comedy winding through the great tragedy of the war. Although it does not have a specific chronological order, the editor has observed a "loose order" of arrangement.

The anthology begins with "Ambuscade," the opening section of Faulkner's novel *The Unvanquished*. This is followed by "The War Years," the opening segment of *The Autobiography of Miss Jane Pittman*, by Earnest Gaines. In "Ambuscade" Bayard Sartoris with his Negro friend Ringo is playing a war game with wood chips. They discover that Federal troops are coming and Bayard views his first Union soldier. In "The War Years" Federal troops arrive at a plantation at which the owner owns slaves. It depicts the predicament of black slaves by relating the actions of a young girl who has been freed. The dilemma of the slaves is whether to remain with their masters or to strike out on their own.

Koon has designated nine stories to comprise the middle of the anthology. This section begins with Mark Twain's "The Private History of a Campaign that Failed." He describes the experience of a group of Missouri volunteers who organize on a lark and then learn that they are truly facing the actual war. Twain's humorous writing makes this story engaging. "The Reign of the Brute," a chapter from Ellen Glasgow's *The Battle-Ground* describes a young Confederate soldier off to his first war experience. Initially, he perceives it as a glorious victory, but he has serious second thoughts as he returns to the battlefield and witnesses a field hospital. *The Long Roll,* by Mary Johnston, is one of the fine novels of the Civil War. "A Woman" is an excerpt from it that takes the reader to Richmond shortly after Federal troops had been turned back for the second time. She offers excellent descriptions of combat through the voices of the wounded who have been brought to an Army hospital.

I was surprised to find an offering by Jack London that deals with the Civil War. "War" describes the irony of Americans both helping and killing each other during the conflict. Ambrose Bierce is a well known author of the War Between the States. In "Killed at Resaca," Bierce tells the story of the death of Lt. Herman Brayle of the Union Army. He describes in interesting fashion the unusual fate of Brayle's last letter.

The collection of stories now turns to more recent work. "The Forest of the South" is by Carolyn Gordon, at one time the wife of the famous writer Allen Tate. Her contribution is an exciting one about romance and deceit across enemy lines. Robert Morgan takes on a different theme. His "Homemade Yankees" relates the actions of renegades and bushwhackers plundering the home front after most of the men have departed for the battlefront. "Dragged Fighting from His Tomb," is from Barry Hannah's collection of short stories entitled Airships (1978) Hannah, currently writer-in-residence at the University of Mississippi, provides us a new version of the well-known death of General Jeb Stuart. "The Burial of the Guns," an old contribution (1894) by the well known writer Thomas Nelson Page, closes the middle section of the anthology. This story deals with the decision of an officer and his men to bury their artillery when they received word of General Lee's surrender.

The editor states that the five stories of the last part of the anthology constitute a type of epilogue. They are set after the war and address in a variety of ways the aftermath of the conflict. "The Return of a Private," by Hamlin Garland, is written from a Northern perspective and depicts the return of Private Ed Smith of Wisconsin from Louisiana after the war. Although Page's Confederates found some glory in their defeat, Smith ironically finds his farm is in ruins and his family separated. One of the most celebrated authors of the Civil War was Stephen Crane, who wrote the splendid novel *The Red Badge of Courage*. In his "The Veteran," Henry Fleming, hero of *The Red Badge of Courage*, concerns his civilian life and death as a veteran after the war.

The book concludes with two stories that inject additional humor into the anthology. One is by O. Henry. He tells the unlikely story of a Yankee attending a Confederate soldiers' convention in "Two Renegades." Fred Chappell, in his lengthy "Ancestors," makes light of the Southern interest in genealogy. The final story is by Flannery O'Connor entitled "A Late Encounter with the Enemy," and tells about the attempts to involve an ancient Civil War soldier, promoted to general in the mind of relatives, in the graduation of his granddaughter. It in effect is a satirical look at the Civil War exploitation in the "New South".

As is quickly discernable, editor Koon has selected a superb group of writers and their stories. This anthology contains little that is new, but it is valuable because it pulls together the works of several important writers dealing with the Civil War. The stories, many of which are unknown to most readers, provide enjoyable reading.

Harris D. Riley, Jr.   Vanderbilt Children's Hospital

*   *   *

BOOKS, BOOKS, BOOKS
A Notice of Recent Publications

We continue the practiced inaugurated in Volume Five, No. 4., of presenting notices of various publications on the American Civil War. This was prompted by the niagra of print on the subject during the past decade and is a way to let readers know about many more volumes than we could review individually. Full reviews will continue to appear as well.

Leading the list is Herman Hattaway's *Shades of Blue And Gray : An Introductory Military History of the Civil War* (University of Missouri Press, Columbia, Missouri, 65201). This is, as the title promises, an "introductory" military history of the war, but it is an excellent one. A product of the author's year-in-residence at West Point as visiting a scholar, it is dedicated to, among others, the cadets who helped inspire it. There are several "pluses." I like the straight-forward style with which Herman presents the military story; the introductory material on military thought prior to the war; and the useful, thorough, and highly personalized opinions in a "Suggested Readings" section that concludes the chapters. This book will be pleasing to lay and professional historians alike; my copy goes beside Joseph Mitchell's *Decisive Battles of the Civil War*, but I expect to reach more for *Shades of Blue and Gray* when I want to check something about a campaign, battle, or military personality.

Douglas L. Wilson's *Honor's Voice: The Transformation of Abraham Lincoln* (Alfred A. Knopf, 201 East Fiftieth St., New York City 10022, $30), deals with the formative years of our sixteenth president. Wilson writes of the early realities rather than the Lincoln Legend so familiar at anelementary level. Wilson's focus is on the period between 1831 and 1842 and on the human aspects of his subject. Then still possessed with the appetites, excesses, and ambitions of youth, Lincoln also exhibited the depression, strained personal relationships, and other difficulties that remained into maturity. Wilson is Saunders Director of the International Center for Jefferson Studies at Monticello; he has produced a thought-provoking examination of the man who led the effort to preserve the Union.

Galveston, Texas, was the gateway to Texas from the Gulf Coast. Union naval forces gained control of the island shortly after the Civil War began, then were forced out by Confederate General John B. Magruder's two-pronged campaign at the beginning of *1863*. *Battle On The Bay: The Civil War Struggle for Galveston*, by Edward T. Cotham, Jr. (University of Texas Press, Box 7819 Austin, Texas, 78713-7819, $37.50 hardcover, $16.95 paperback), tells the story of this barrier-island port city, blockade center, and Civil War fortress. Emphasis is placed on the crucial battle to reclaim Galveston from Union control; once this was accomplished, Confederates retained control of the island until the end of the war. Cotham is a resident of Houston, which is located north of Galveston on Buffalo Bayou, and is a former president of the Houston Civil War Round Table.

Texas A&M Press has rescued Alwyn Barr's *Polignac's Texas Brigade* (Texas A&M Press, John H. Lindsey Building, Lewis Street, College Station, Texas 77843-4354, $12.96 paper). Published in 1964 by the Gulf Coast Historical Association with a limited press run, this major university press now makes this interesting study of the brigade led by Camille Armand Jules Marie, Prince de Polignac—or "Pole-Cat" to his rough-cut command of 5,000 men mostly raised in North Texas. Composed of three cavalry regiments, the brigade was dismounted, to the embarrassment and chagrin of all involved, but fought valiantly in various actions in Louisiana (Stirling's Plantation, Bayou Bourbeau, and Sabine Crossroads), Arkansas (Prairie Grove), and Missouri (Shirley's Ford and Newtonia). Barr, a professor at Texas Tech University, was among the first to discuss the Red River Campaign; he has added a new preface for this edition.

Also associated, at least partially, with Louisiana, is Chester G. Hearn's *When The Devil Came Down To Dixie: Ben Butler in New Orleans* (Louisiana State University Press, Box 25053, Baton Rouge, Louisiana 70894-5053, $26.95). Not a classic biography—Butler's "Early Years" are handled in an introductory chapter of that title—this volume concentrates on Butler military rather than his political career, especially his occupation of the Crescent City. Georgians and Carolinians had their William T. Sherman to blame for all wartime and postwar calamities, and Louisianaians, especially those from New Orleans, had their own special devil in the person of "Spoons"/"Beast" Butler. A more neutral examination might judge his administration of New Orleans not so bad, but generations of Louisianians nurtured their contempt for Butler as an article of faith. My favorite anechdote: Butler's "woman order" so irritated genuine prostitutes who resented his order's association of amateurs with their profession that they had his portrait painted on the bottom of their chamber pots to receive a periodic expression of their opinion of him. Butler wasn't as bad as some political appointees, even if he wasn't as good a commander as he should have been. This is a modern review of his Civil War career that merits the attention of those interested in this part of the war. Hearn is the author of a number of Civil War books, including *The Capture of New Orleans, 1862.*

Looking at another port city, Thomas H. O'Connor examines the impact of conflict in *Civil War Boston: Home Front & Battlefield* (Northeastern University Press, 360 Huntington Avenue, 416CP, Boston, Massachusetts 02115, $26.95). Far removed from the battle line, Bostonians nevertheless were affected by the Civil War. O'Connor features the changes the war brought to the businessmen, Irish Catholic immigrants, blacks, and women of Boston. It is a city study and so will be of greatest interest to urban historians and those involved with the featured city. O'Connor is an emeritus professor of history at Boston College and the author of a number of other books on Boston.

Now for some soldiers: Larry B. Maier's *Rough & Regular: A History of Philadelphia's 119th Regiment of Pennsylvania Volunteer Infantry, The Gray Reserves* (Burd Street Press, Division of White Mane Publishing Company, Box 152, Shippensburg, Pennsylvania 17257-0152, $30.00), pretty wells tells you what this book is about in the longest title imaginable. This regiment was involved in every campaign of the Army of the Potomac as part of the 3rd Brigade, 1st Division, Sixth Corps. The bulk of Maier's book is a narrative of the brigade's experiences, but some might find Appendix A, the roster of the 119th, to be of greatest use. Each member of the regiment is identified by name, rank, company assignment, enlistment or conscription and discharge date, and "Remarks" such as "mustered out," "died," "deserted," "transferred," or, more solemnly, "lost leg is action." Maier is an attorney in Ephrata, Pennsylvania, who toured every battlefield where the 199th fought.

And more soldiers: Edward A. Miller, Jr., *The Black Civil War Soldiers of Illinois* (University of South Carolina Press, 937 Assembly Street, Carolina Plaza, 8th Floor, Columbia, South Carolina 29208, $29.95) follows the path of the 29th U.S. Colored Infantry, one of nearly 150 regiments/batteries composed of black troops, and the only one from Illinois. Miller examined pension records, regimental papers, reports, and correspondence to learn, and then tell, the story of individual soldiers. The illustrations are good but all bunched in one place. No roster. Miller was a career officer in the Air Force and afterwards had a successful business career. He previously authored biographies of David Hunter and Robert Smalls.

Robert E. Lee continues to attract the attention of historians, now in Bevin Alexander's *Robert E. Lee's Civil War* (Adams Media Corporation, 260 Center Street, Holbrook, Massachusetts 02343 $24.95), released in May 1998, and J. Tracy Power's *Lee's Miserables: Life In The Army of Northern Virginia From The*

Wilderness To Appomattox (University of North Carolina Press, Box 2288, Chapel Hill, North Carolina 27515-2288, R.34.95), due in April 1998. We are working from uncorrected page proofs in both cases, but the edge goes to Alexander's book because Adams Media sent along the jacket and corrected pages for chaper 11, "Gettysburg." This book promises a "vivid depiction" of battles and a "prevocative re-examination" of the military mind of Lee. It gives Lee credit for good defensive maneuvers and for holding together his underequipped army. Alexander lives in Richmond, Virginia, and is the author of other works on military history. Power's book is about Lee's army more that the man himself, but obviously he is a major figure. The soldiers identified with the meaning in Hugo's *Les Miserables*, making it into "Lees Miserables," their own story of difficult. Sources primarily are the diaries and letters of the soldiers themselves. Power is a historian employed by the South Carolina Department of Archives and History in Columbia.

As usual, there is also much interest in Gettysburg. Comes now another book on that subject edited by Gabor S. Boritt, director of the Civil War Institute and Fluher Professor at Gettysburg College. *The Gettysburg Nobody Knows* (Oxford University Press, New York—Business Office, 2001 Evans Road, Cary, North Carolina 27513, $27.50), is dedicated "To The Students Of The Gettysburg Civil War Institute, Past, Present, and Future." Boritt corraled the following scholars to visit the Institute, and here gives us the literary evidence of their presentations: Joseph T. Glatthaar, "The Common Soldier's Gettysburg Campaign;" Glenn LaFantasie, "Joshua Chamberlain and the American Dream;" Harry W. Pfanz, "'Old Jack' Is Not Here;" Kent Gramm, "The Chances of War: Lee, Longstreet, Sickles, and the First Minnesota Volunteers;" Emory M. Thomas, "Eggs, Aldie, Shepherdstown, and J. E. B. Stuart;" Carol Reardon, "'I Think the Union Army Had Something To Do With It'": The Pickett's Charge Nobody Knows;" J. Matthew Gallman with Susan Baker, "Gettysburg's Gettysburg: What the Battle Did to the Borough;" Richard M. McMurry, "The Pennsylvania Gambit and the Gettysburg Splash;" and Amy J. Kinsel, "From Turning Point to Peace Memorial: A Cultural Legacy." Even so, there will be more on Gettysburg.

Such as James M. McPherson's and Patricia R. McPherson's *Lamson of the Gettysburg: The Civil War Letters of Lieutenant Roswell H. Lamson, U.S. Navy* (Oxford University Press, see above for address, $25). Except this Gettysburg is a boat, not a battle, and the book is composed of the letters of its commander. This will be of special interest to students of the naval war. James McPherson is the author of *Battle Cry of Freedom* and other well-known works on the war; Patricia McPherson is his wife and an independent researcher.

Sticking with the naval army, R. Thomas Campbell's *Fire & Thunder: Exploits of the Confederate States Navy* (Burd Street Press, Division of White Mane Publishing Company, Box 152, Shippensburg, Pennsylvania 17257-0152, $24.95) discusses various aspects of the Confederate effort afloat, including privateers, the Mosquito Fleet, the naval war at New Orleans and Galveston, blockade runners, and on the high seas every where. If this is the kind of thing you like, then this is the kind of thing you will like.

Dr. Archie P. McDonald   Stephen F. Austin State University

INDEX

We are pleased to announce the release of an important new Civil War reference work. . .

THE GENERALS OF GETTYSBURG:

An Encyclopedia of the Leaders of America's Greatest Battle,

by Larry Tagg

Author Tagg's study is a useful, insightful, and entertaining new contribution to the literature of the Civil War in the East. *The Generals of Gettysburg* includes a detailed biographical listing of each brigade-level (or higher) commander from both armies, together with a picture of each officer. Organized for easy reference by Corps, Divisions, and brigades, each listing contains an in-depth examination of his pre-Gettysburg experience, a full discussion of his service at Gettysburg, and a brief discussion of his life after the battle. Each entry is followed with a suggested reading list.

Accompanied by John Heiser's cartography, *The Generals of Gettysburg* belongs on every Civil War student's bookshelf. Available at bookstores everywhere, or call 1-800-732-3669 for your copy today.

* * *

Below are pair of sample entries, one Union and one Confederate, from *The Generals of Gettysburg:*

SECOND BRIGADE: 1,333 men

Brigadier General Adelbert Ames

General Ames was young for a brigadier general, only twenty-eight at Gettysburg. He was originally a clipper seaman, but he received an appointment to West Point from his native Maine. Ames graduated 5th out of 45 students in the Class of 1861, which completed its studies just after the fall of Fort Sumter. He was assigned to the artillery and fought at Bull Run only two months after graduating, where he was badly wounded in the right thigh. He refused to leave his guns until he was too weak to remain seated on a caisson. (For this heroic performance Ames received a Congressional Medal of Honor in 1893.) Returning to duty, he fought in the Peninsula Campaign the next summer, seeing action at Yorktown,

Gaines' Mill and Malvern Hill, where his conduct was referred to as "above praise" by the brilliant and respected Col. Henry Hunt, chief of the Artillery Reserve of the Army of the Potomac.

Ames realized that he could advance in rank more quickly in the volunteer infantry, so he returned to Maine to campaign for a command. State officials were only too happy to indulge the talented young officer, and in August 1862, he became colonel of the 20th Maine Volunteers, an outfit destined for immortality the next year at Gettysburg. Ames led the 20th in the Maryland Campaign, but it was kept in reserve with the rest of the Federal Fifth Corps at the Battle of Antietam. At Fredericksburg in December, Ames led his regiment in one of the last charges of the day against Marye's Heights. It ended, like all the others, in failure, but mercifully only 36 men in the regiment became casualties. During the Chancellorsville Campaign in May 1863, Colonel Ames—with an eye toward his own advancement—temporarily relinquished command of his regiment to volunteer as an aide to Fifth Corps commander Maj. Gen. George Meade. On the 20th of May, two weeks after Chancellorsville, Ames received a promotion to brigadier general out of respect for his military talent.

(Staff duty with Meade seemed to have this effect on young West Pointers' careers, for staff officer Alexander Webb also became a general at this time).The commander of the Eleventh Corps, Maj. Gen. Oliver Howard, brought Ames and Brig. Gen. Francis Barlow into his First Division to improve the discipline and fighting abilities of his men after their disastrous experience at Chancellorsville. Ames handed over command of the 20th Maine to an obscure colonel named Col. Joshua Chamberlain, and took over the leadership of his brigade.

Artilleryman Charles Wainwright found Ames "the best kind of a man to be associated with, cool and clear in his own judgment, gentlemanly and without the smallest desire to interfere."Furthermore, mused Wainwright, "strange thing in this army, I did not hear him utter an oath of any kind [for] three days!"

Ames was new to his brigade and brigade-level command. In fact, the Battle of Fredericksburg was the only occasion upon which he had commanded infantry in combat. Even with such handicaps, he was a talented professional officer and was expected to do well in any situation.

GETTYSBURG: Ames' brigade marched in column behind von Gilsa's out of Gettysburg, crossed over the Carlisle Road to the Harrisburg Road, and was massed east of the road behind a small ridge upon which sat the county Almshouse. The regiments, aligned in double column of companies, were deployed right to left as follows: 107th and 25th Ohio regiment, 17th Connecticut, and the 75th Ohio in support. The massive enemy buildup opposite Col.

Leopold von Gilsa's thinly-spread brigade on Blocher's Knoll prompted Barlow to deploy Ames' brigade 400 yards north of the Almshouse in support. The 25th Ohio took up a position on the knoll, and the 107th formed on its left, facing northwest. The remaining two regiments were massed in the rear as Barlow's sole divisional reserve.

Soon after 3:00 p.m., von Gilsa was struck from two directions and knocked off the field, exposing Ames' right flank. Brig. Gen. John B. Gordon's Georgians smashed into it, collapsing the 25th and 107th Ohio regiments, and Ames ordered up his two reserve regiments. "It was a fearful advance and made at a dreadful cost of life," remembered the 75th Ohio leader, Col. Andrew Harris. Colonel von Gilsa's retreating men made it difficult for Ames' regiments to stand and fight, and they too were soon driven from Blocher's Knoll. While attempting to rally his division, General Barlow fell with a serious wound, and the youthful Ames inherited command of the division at a time when it was "falling back with little or no regularity, regimental organizations having become destroyed." Ames and von Gilsa established a new defensive line near the Almshouse, but two more fresh Southern brigades attacked it, forcing a general retreat.

The retreat continued through the streets of Gettysburg and up Cemetery Hill, where Ames' regiments were reorganized on the northeast face, east of the Baltimore Pike. Ames' brigade (led now by Colonel Harris) formed in an L-shaped defensive line, with the shank (17th Connecticut and 25th Ohio) along the Brickyard Lane facing northeast, and the 107th and 25th Ohio regiments forming the bottom of the "L" facing north.

On July 2, this position was struck head-on at dusk by Hays' Louisiana Brigade, which swept Ames' regiments from the crest of the hill. The timely arrival of Col. Samuel Carroll's Second Corps brigade, together with elements from Ames' and von Gilsa's brigades, managed to push the unsupported Confederates off the hill and save the important position. When things quieted down, Carroll requested support for his exposed brigade. Ames replied that his own troops were rattled, and asked Carroll to remain in his front. The fiery Carroll shot back, "Damn a man who [has] no confidence in his troops." The northeast face of Cemetery Hill was not attacked again during the fighting.

Two weeks after the battle, Brig. Gen. George Gordon replaced Ames at the head of the division and took the command to South Carolina, while Ames reverted to command of his brigade. He served the rest of the war in brigade and division commands in various theaters.

Ames was assigned to duty in Mississippi after the war and was made military, then provisional governor there. He was elected to as U.S. Senator from that state in 1870, then reelected governor of Mississippi in 1874. His administration was beset by race riots and official misconduct, and he resigned in 1876 to avoid impeachment. Ames was the last Civil War general to die, in 1933.

For further reading:

Benson, Harry K. "The Public Career of Adelbert Ames, 1861-1876," Thesis, Univ. of VA, 1975.

Hartwig, D. Scott. "The 11th Army Corps on July 1." *Gettysburg Magazine*, #2, 1990.

Pfanz, Harry W. *Gettysburg: Culp's Hill and Cemetery Hill*. Chapel Hill. 1993.

ARCHER'S BRIGADE

(The "Tennessee Brigade"): 1,193 men

Brigadier General
James Jay Archer

James Archer, a native of the northern Maryland town of Bel Air, was forty-five years old at Gettysburg. He attended Princeton University, where he was tagged with the unusual nickname of "Sally."There is some conjecture about Archer's sexual orientation. While some writers point to his feminine nickname as an indication that he was homosexual, Confederate diarist Mary Chesnut mentioned that Archer was a classmate of her husband's, and according to Mr. Chesnut, "in Princeton College they called him Sally Archer, he was so pretty when he entered." Evidently Archer's smooth, delicate features and slight build accounted for the moniker. Others, however, mention that after his capture at Gettysburg, he played female rolls in the skits put on by the prisoners at Johnson's Island prison camp; Archer though, was slight of build, even frail, and those parts probably fell to him solely for that reason. There is also the testimony of one North Carolinian that at Johnson's Island, after a dinner party,"Capt. Taylor got some whiskey. . .& he had Gen. Archer down & they all got drink together & got to hugging each other & saying that they had slept together many a time." The observer is probably describing nothing more than drunken reminiscing by old army buddies, and it was common for soldiers to huddle together at night, or "spoon," for warmth during cold-weather campaigns. Archer never married, and was not comfortable in the presence of single women. A friend once described the general as "timid and retiring" socially. The only women known to be in his life were his sister and mother.

After graduating in 1835, Archer studied law at the University of Maryland and was admitted to the bar. He practiced law until the Mexican War began in 1846, when he joined the Regular Army as a captain of infantry and received a brevet for gallantry at the Battle of Chapultapec. His only wound was suffered in a duel with a fellow officer. (Archer's "second" in the duel was his friend Thomas J. Jackson.) After the war with Mexico was over, he went back to his law practice, then reentered the Regular Army in 1855, again as an infantry captain.

On March 14, 1861, he resigned his commission and received a captaincy in the new Confederate army. He was stationed in Fort Walla Walla in Washington Territory, and had to travel overland to reach the Confederacy. In October he was appointed colonel of the 5th Texas regiment, which was organized in Richmond from independent companies that had made their way to the Southern capital from the Lone Star State.

Archer's regiment was brigaded with other Texas regiments under the leadership of Col. John B. Hood and sent to the Peninsula the following spring. With no real battle experience, Archer was plucked from his regiment (where he had not endeared himself to the Texans, who thought him a tyrant) and promoted to brigadier general on June 3, 1861. He took command of three Tennessee regiments after their brigadier was killed in the Battle of Seven Pines. The Tennesseans didn't initially take to Archer any more than the Texans had. "His temper was irascible, and so cold was his manner that we thought him at first a Martinet," wrote one of the soldiers. He was "very non-communicative, the bearing and extreme reserve of the old army officer made him, for a time, one of the most hated of men."

Archer's Brigade was combined with five others later in the month to form a new division—grandly styled the "Light Division"—under the command of Maj. Gen. A. P. Hill. Archer's first combat at the head of his brigade came in the Seven Days' Battles at Mechanicsville, where the brigade was repulsed while assaulting a strong Union position. This frustration was followed by the bloodshed at Gaines' Mill, where Archer's Brigade plunged to within mere yards of the Union line before being driven back with heavy losses. His actions on the field, though, changed the attitude of his men:

No sooner, however, had he led his brigade through the first Richmond campaign. than quite a evolution took place in sentiment . . .He had none of the politician or aristocrat, but never lost the dignity or bearing of an officer. While in battle he seemed the very God of war, and every inch a soldier according to its strictest rules. . . . He won the hearts of his men by his won-

derful judgment and conduct on the field, and they had the most implicit confidence in him. He was dubbed "The Little Game Cock."

Shifted to Stonewall Jackson's command in front of Maj. Gen. John Pope's Union army, Archer and his men performed competently at the Battle of Cedar Mountain in August. At the climactic defeat of Pope at Second Manassas, Archer's men saw heavy fighting in defense of the Railroad Cut, and Archer's horse was shot out from under him. In the Maryland Campaign, after the reduction of Harpers Ferry, Archer fell sick on the hard march to rejoin the main army at Sharpsburg and turned the brigade over to a subordinate. As the Light Division deployed to attack, he climbed out of his ambulance and resumed command, though he could barely stay in the saddle. According to A. P. Hill, "My troops were not a minute too soon. . .With a yell of defiance, Archer charged [the enemy]. . . and drove them back pell-mell." Spearheading the attack that probably saved Robert E. Lee's Army of Northern Virginia proved to be the climax of Archer's Civil War career. The next morning, his remaining strength completely exhausted by the previous day's effort, he relinquished command again and returned to his sickbed.

At Fredericksburg, Hill's divisional line was deployed with a 500-yard gap between the left of Archer's Brigade and the right of James Lanes' North Carolinians. This area, marshy and deemed impenetrable, was attacked by Maj. Gen. George Meade's division, which drove through it and threatened to rupture the Confederate front. Archer, again coming off sick leave on the day of the battle, proved himself equal to the crisis, bending back his line so that it remained firing as the Yankees stormed through the opening. He was in the thick of the action, cutting at enemy soldiers with his heavy saber, and for a moment was engaged in a violent struggle with a Federal who held the bridle of his rearing black mare. Brig. Gen. Jubal Early, whose men came to Archer's aid, praised Archer after the fight, writing, "I feel it incumbent upon me to state that to Brigadier-General Archer. . .is due the credit of having held the enemy in check, with a small portion of his men, after his flank and rear had been gained . . .But for the gallant stand made by General Archer the enemy would have gained an advantage which it would have required a greater sacrifice of life to wrest from him than was made."

Archer also served well during the May 1863 Chancellorsville Campaign. His brigade was near the tail of Maj. Gen. Thomas "Stonewall" Jackson's long flanking column. When the rear of the column was attacked by men from Maj. Gen. Dan Sickles' Third Corps, Archer took it upon himself to turn his and Brig. Gen. Ed Thomas' brigade around to repulse the Federals. His action caused him to miss the assault that evening, which routed the Federal Eleventh Corps. Though he had not cleared his decision with a superior, there is no evidence that Archer was reprimanded. He helped capture the strategically crucial high ground at Hazel Grove the following day, and General Lee later rode up to Archer's Brigade, a move which signaled the reunification of the Army of Northern Virginia. Because of a secession of wounds, Archer ended up leading the Light Division in the latter stages of the battle.

His own writings and the testimony of men who knew him make it clear that Archer—despite his Princeton education—was not an especially clever man. He was, however, a proven combat leader. As he approached Gettysburg in the vanguard of Hill's Third Corps on July 1, he had the self-assurance that came with the knowledge that there was very little the enemy could show him that he had not already seen over the last year of war.

GETTYSBURG: Archer's was the lead brigade of Maj. Gen. Henry Heth's Division as it marched toward Gettysburg along the Chambersburg Pike on July 1. Since he expected to find enemy cavalry on the road, he was not unprepared when, around 7:30 a.m., Union troopers were spotted and the first shots rang out. Confederate skirmishers slowly pushed the horsemen (Colonel Gamble's troopers) past Herr Ridge over the next hour and a half. As the Federal defense began to stiffen, division commander Henry Heth deployed Archer's Brigade on the right (south) side of the Chambersburg Pike and Brig. Gen. Joseph Davis' Brigade left of the roadway. Archer's regiments were deployed, from left to right, as follows: 7th, 14th and 1st Tennessee and 13th Alabama.

About 9:30 a.m., Heth ordered Archer and Davis forward to drive the pesky cavalry away once and for all. Archer presciently protested, suggesting that his brigade should not be pushed so far forward of any support; Heth insisted, however, and Archer's regiments started across the shallow valley which dipped down to Willoughby Run and up to McPherson's Ridge. Artillery shells plastered the men almost immediately. When the battle line slowly ascended the wooded ridge to the east, however, it was surprised by the appearance of the black-hatted veterans of Solomon Meredith's Iron Brigade, who were just arriving over the ridge crest. This situation was just the sort of thing Archer had warned Heth against. As bristling lines of muskets roared and crackled, the right, then the left of Archer's Brigade fell back to Willoughby Run some yards to the rear.

Heavy fighting followed, and before long, Archer's right collapsed completely, the left followed suit, and the entire brigade was streaming for the rear. Although pockets of the resistance formed here and there in an attempt to make a stand, the early morning march, earlier fight—and the shock of meeting elite veteran troops instead of dismounted cavalry—sealed the doom of Archer's Brigade on July 1.Those not fleet enough of foot were taken captive. Among them was General Archer, who was sick with a fever for the third time in his last four battles. Too weak to run, Archer—the first of Lee's generals captured in battle—was caught just thirty paces west of the creek by Pvt. Patrick Mahoney of the 2nd Wisconsin. For him, the battle and the war were over.

Archer was marched away the next day and eventually confined on Johnson's Island in Ohio for about a year. He was exchanged in August 1864, but the sickly general died of general debilitation and exhaustion two months later.

Archer's Brigade, now under the command of Col. Birkett D. Fry, was held in reserve on July 2, but was thrown into the maelstrom of Pickett's Charge on the last day of the battle. The weak brigade, which by that time probably mustered about half of what it did on July 1, suffered heavily in the assault.

For further reading:

"Brigadier General James T. Archer." *Confederate Veteran*, 8, no. 2, 1900.

Martin, David. *Gettysburg: July 1*. Combined Books, 1996.

Schenck, Martin. *Up Came Hill: The Story of the Light Division and its Leaders*. Harrisburg, 1958.

Storch, Marc & Beth. "'What a Deadly Trap We Were In': Archer's Brigade on July 1, 1863." *Gettysburg Magazine*, #6, 1992.

The Generals of Gettysburg: An Encyclopedia of the Leaders of America's Greatest Battle, by Larry Tagg. Specifications: cloth, d.j., 450pp., maps, photos, $29.95. Published by Savas Publishing Co., 1475 S. Bascom Ave., Suite 204, Campbell, CA 95008.

Distributed into the trade by Stackpole Books, 5067 Ritter Road, Mechanicsburg, PA 17055. Order toll free by calling 1-800-732-3669.